Eyewitness
WORLD WAR I

Early British reconnaissance aircraft

Signpost from Ypres station, 1916

Book that stopped a bullet

Early gas helmet

British "carcass" incendiary bomb

British 20 lb (9 kg) Hales bomb

French tin soldiers

German incendiary bomb, dropped during first air raid on London

Model of British motor ambulance used on the Western Front

Prussian Iron
Cross

Eyewitness
WORLD
WAR I

US Distinguished
Service Cross

Written by
SIMON ADAMS

Photographed by
ANDY CRAWFORD

British Maxim Mark 3
machine gun

Figurine of
Herbert Asquith,
British prime
minister from
1908 to 1916

Figurine of Grand
Duke Nicolas,
commander-in-
chief of the Russian
armies at the start
of the war

DK Publishing

British officer's compass

German steel helmet adapted for use with a telephone

Dummy rifles used by British army recruits, 1914–15

French *Croix de Guerre* medal awarded for valor

British and German barbed wire

British steel helmet with visor

Grenade

German medical orderly's pouch

DK

LONDON, NEW YORK, MELBOURNE, MUNICH, and DELHI

Project editor Patricia Moss
Art editors Julia Harris, Rebecca Painter
Senior editor Monica Byles
Senior art editors Jane Tetzlaff, Clare Shedden
Category publisher Jayne Parsons
Managing art editor Jacquie Gulliver
Senior production controller Kate Oliver
Picture research Sean Hunter
DTP designers Justine Eaton, Matthew Ibbotson

THIS EDITION
Editor Sue Nicholson
Managing editor Camilla Hallinan
Managing art editor Martin Wilson
Publishing manager Sunita Gahir
Category publisher Andrea Pinnington
Production editors Andy Hilliard,
Laragh Kedwell, Hitesh Patel
Production controller Georgina Hayworth
U.S. editors Margaret Parrish, John Searcy

This Eyewitness ® Guide has been conceived by
Dorling Kindersley Limited and Editions Gallimard

This edition first published in the United States in 2007
by DK Publishing, 375 Hudson Street, New York, NY 10014

A catalog record for this book is available
from the Library of Congress.

ISBN 978-0-7566-3007-2 (HC) 978-0-7566-0741-8 (Library Binding)

Color reproduction by Colourscan, Singapore
Printed by Toppan Printing Co. (Shenzhen) Ltd., China

Discover more at
www.dk.com

Contents

6
Divided Europe
8
The fatal shot
10
War in the west
12
Fighting men
14
Joining up
16
Digging the trenches
18
Life in the trenches
20
Ready to fight
22
Communication and supplies
24
Observation and patrol
26
Bombardment
28
Over the top
30
Casualty
32
Women at war
34
War in the air
36
Zeppelin
38
War at sea
40
Gallipoli
42
Verdun

44
Gas attack
46
The Eastern Front
48
War in the desert
50
Espionage
52
Tank warfare
54
The US enters the war
56
Under enemy lines
58
The final year
60
Armistice and peace
62
The cost of the war
64
Did you know?
66
Key people and places
68
Find out more
70
Glossary
72
Index

High
explosive
shells

Divided Europe

AT THE START of the 20th century, the countries of Europe were increasingly hostile to each other. Britain, France, and Germany competed for trade and influence overseas, while Austria-Hungary and Russia both tried to dominate the Balkan states of southeast Europe. Military tension between Germany and Austria-Hungary, on the one hand, and Russia and France, on the other, led to the formation of powerful military alliances. A naval arms race added to the tension. In 1912–13 two major wars broke out in the Balkans as rival states battled to divide Turkish-controlled lands between them. By 1914 the political situation in Europe was tense, but few believed that a continental war was inevitable.

HMS DREADNOUGHT
The launch of HMS *Dreadnought* in February 1906 marked a revolution in battleship design. With its 10 12-inch (30-cm) guns and a top speed of 21 knots, the British ship outperformed and outpaced every other battleship of the day. As a result, Germany, France, and other maritime nations began to design and build their own battleships, starting a worldwide naval armaments race.

KAISER WILHELM II
Wilhelm II became emperor of Germany in 1888, when he was just 29. He had a withered arm and other disabilities, but overcame them through his strong personality. As emperor, he tried to turn Germany from a European power into a world power, but his aggressive policies and arrogant behavior upset other European nations, particularly Britain and France.

Some children had models of HMS Dreadnought and could recite every detail of her statistics

Handpainted, tinplate toy battleship

EUROPEAN RIVALRIES

In 1882 Germany, Austria-Hungary, and Italy signed the Triple Alliance to protect themselves against invasion. Alarmed by this, France and Russia formed an alliance in 1894. Britain signed ententes (understandings) with France in 1904 and Russia in 1907. During the war, Serbia, Montenegro, Belgium, Romania, Portugal, and Greece fought with the Allies. Bulgaria and Turkey fought alongside Germany and Austria-Hungary—the Central Powers. Italy joined the Allies in 1915.

■ Central Powers
■ Allied Nations
■ Neutral

A FAMILY AFFAIR?

Although George V and Czar Nicholas II look very similar, they were not directly related. Nicholas's wife, Alexandra, however, was a cousin of George V, as was Emperor Wilhelm of Germany.

Czar Nicholas II of Russia   George V of Britain

THE GERMAN FLEET

In 1898 Germany began an ambitious naval building program designed to challenge the supremacy of the British Royal Navy. While German admirals commanded these new ships in the Baltic and North Seas, German children played with tin battleships in their bathtubs.

Key to wind up clockwork motor

THE POWER HOUSE

The factory, shown above, in the Ruhr valley of western Germany belonged to the Alfred Krupp Arms Company. The Krupp family was the largest arms supplier in the world. Germany was a largely agricultural nation when it became a united country in 1871. Over the next 30 years, new iron, coal, steel, engineering, and shipbuilding industries turned Germany into the third biggest industrial country in the world, after the US and Britain.

The fatal shot

THE ASSASSINS
Gavrilo Princip, above right, fired the fatal shot. He belonged to the Black Hand terrorists, who believed that Bosnia should be part of Serbia.

O N JUNE 28, 1914, the heir to the Austro-Hungarian throne, Archduke Franz Ferdinand, was assassinated in Sarajevo, Bosnia. Bosnia had been part of Austria-Hungary since 1908, but it was claimed by neighboring Serbia. Austria-Hungary blamed Serbia for the assassination, and on July 28 declared war. What began as the third Balkan war within two years turned into a European war. Russia supported Serbia, Germany supported Austria-Hungary, and France supported Russia. On August 4, Germany invaded neutral Belgium on its way to France. It intended to knock France out of the war before turning its attention to Russia, thus avoiding war on two fronts. But Britain had guaranteed to defend Belgium's neutrality, and it too declared war on Germany. The Great War had begun.

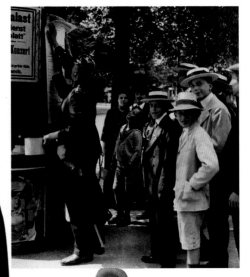

THE AUSTRO-HUNGARIAN ARMY
The Austro-Hungarian empire had three armies—Austrian, Hungarian, and the "Common Army." Ten main languages were spoken! The official one was German, but officers had to learn their men's language, leading to frequent communication difficulties. The complex structure of the army reflected Austria-Hungary itself, which in reality was two separate monarchies ruled by one monarch.

MOBILIZE!
During July 1914, military notices were posted up across Europe informing citizens that their country's army was being mobilized (prepared) for war and that all those belonging to regular and reserve forces should report for duty.

GERMANY REJOICES
Germany prepared its army on August 1, declaring war against Russia later the same evening and against France on August 3. Most Germans in the cities were enthusiastic for the war and many civilians rushed to join the army in support of Kaiser and country. Germans in the countryside were less enthusiastic.

Austro-Hungarian *Reiter* (Trooper) of the 8th Uhlan (Lancer) Regiment

Bomb bounced off canopy and landed under following car

Archduke and his wife Sophie sat in the back of the open-top car

Princip fired at close range from the running board

ONE DAY IN SARAJEVO
The six assassins—five Serbs and one Bosnian Muslim—lay in wait along Archduke Ferdinand's route to the Austrian governor's residence in Sarajevo. One of them threw a bomb at Ferdinand's car, but it bounced off and exploded under the following car, injuring two army officers. The Archduke and his wife went to visit the injured officers in the hospital 45 minutes later. When their car took a wrong turning, Gavrilo Princip stepped out of the crowd and shot the couple. Ferdinand's wife died instantly and he died 10 minutes later.

June 28 Archduke Franz Ferdinand is assassinated in Sarajevo
July 5 Germany gives its ally Austria-Hungary total support for any action it takes against Serbia

July 23 Austria issues a drastic ultimatum to Serbia, which would undermine Serbian independence
July 25 Serbia agrees to most of

Austria-Hungary's demands, but still mobilizes as a safety precaution.
July 28 Austria-Hungary ignores Serbia's readiness to seek a peaceful

end to the crisis and declares war
July 30 Russia mobilizes in support of its ally, Serbia
July 31 Germany demands that Russia stop its mobilization

German (above) and French (right) mobilization posters

VIVE LA FRANCE
The French army mobilized on August 1. For many Frenchmen, the war was an opportunity to seek revenge for the German defeat of France in 1870–71 and the loss of Alsace-Lorraine to German control.

ALL ABOARD!
The German slogans on this westbound train read "Day trip to Paris" and "See you again on the Boulevard," since all Germans believed that their offensive against France would soon take them to Paris. French trains heading east toward Germany carried similar messages about Berlin.

> *"The lamps are going out all over Europe"*
> SIR EDWARD GREY
> BRITISH FOREIGN SECRETARY, 1914

August 1 Germany mobilizes against Russia and declares war; France mobilizes in support of its ally, Russia; Germany signs a treaty with Ottoman Turkey; Italy declares its neutrality
August 2 Germany invades Luxembourg and demands the right to enter neutral Belgium, which is refused
August 3 Germany declares war on France
August 4 Germany invades Belgium on route to France; Britain enters the war to safeguard Belgian neutrality
August 6 Austria-Hungary declares war on Russia
August 12 France and Britain declare war on Austria-Hungary

War in the west

Ever since the 1890s, Germany had feared that it would face a war on two fronts—against Russia in the east and against France, Russia's ally since 1894, in the west. Germany knew the chances of winning such a war were slim. By 1905, the chief of the German staff, Field Marshal Count Alfred von Schlieffen, had developed a bold plan to knock France swiftly out of any war before turning the full might of the German army against Russia. For this plan to work, the German army had to pass through Belgium, a neutral country. In August 1914, the plan went into operation. German troops crossed the Belgian border on August 4, and by the end of the month, invaded northern France. The Schlieffen Plan then required the army to sweep around the north and west of Paris, but the German commander, General Moltke, modified the plan and instead headed east of Paris. This meant his right flank (side) was exposed to the French and British armies. At the Battle of the Marne on September 5, the German advance was held and pushed back. By Christmas 1914, the two sides faced stalemate along a line from the Belgian coast in the north to the Swiss border in the south.

IN RETREAT
The Belgian army was too small and inexperienced to resist the invading German army. Here, soldiers with dog-drawn machine guns are withdrawing to Antwerp.

IN THE FIELD
The British Expeditionary Force (B.E.F.) had arrived in France by August 22, 1914. Its single cavalry division included members of the Royal Horse Artillery, whose L Battery fired this 13-pounder quick firing Mark I gun against the German 4th Cavalry Division at the Battle of Néry on September 1. This held up the German advance into France for one morning. Three gunners in the battery received Victoria Crosses for their valor.

Third gunner fires the gun on command

Second gunner loads the shell

First gunner hands shell to second gunner on command

Steel helmet

Shaft to attach gun to horses that pull the gun along

Soldiers wore puttees, long strips of cloth wrapped around their legs

THE CHRISTMAS TRUCE

On Christmas Eve, 1914, soldiers on both sides of the Western Front sang carols to each other in comradely greeting. The following day, troops along two-thirds of the front observed a truce. All firing stopped, and church services were held. A few soldiers crossed into no-man's-land to talk to their enemy and exchange simple gifts of cigarettes and other items. Opposite Ploegsteert Wood, south of Ypres, Belgium, a game of soccer took place between members of the German Royal Saxon Regiment and the Scottish Seaforth Highlanders. The Germans won 3–2. In some places, the truce lasted for almost a week. A year later, however, sentries on both sides were ordered to shoot anyone attempting a repeat performance.

Soldier shooting at enemy with a note saying "Christmas Eve—Get 'em!"

British and German soldiers greeting each other on Christmas Day

EYEWITNESS

Captain E. R. P. Berryman of the 2nd Battalion 39th Garwhal Rifles of the Indian Army wrote a letter home describing the truce. He told his family that the Germans had put up Christmas trees in their trenches. This cartoon illustrates the absurdity of his situation—shooting the enemy one day and greeting them as friends the next.

German trench

Rope wrapped around recoil mechanism

Fires 12½-lb (5.6-kg) shells a distance of 5,900 yards (5,395 m)

HEADING FOR THE FRONT

The German advance into northern France was so rapid that by early September, its troops were along the Marne River, only 25 miles (40 km) east of Paris. General Gallieni, military governor of Paris, took 600 taxis and used them to convey 6,000 men to the front line to reinforce the French 6th Army.

Fighting men

THE OUTBREAK OF WAR in Europe in August 1914 changed the lives of millions of men. Regular soldiers, older reservists, eager recruits, and unwilling conscripts all found themselves caught up in the war. Some of them were experienced soldiers, but many had barely held a rifle before. In addition to the European forces, both Britain and France drew heavily on armies recruited from their overseas colonies and from the British dominions. The design and detail of their uniforms differed considerably, although brighter colors soon gave way to khaki, dull blue, and gray.

France

GRAND DUKE NICOLAS
At the outbreak of war, the Russian army was led by Grand Duke Nicolas, uncle of Czar Nicholas II. In August 1915, the czar dismissed his uncle and took command himself. As commander-in-chief, the czar dealt with the overall strategy of the war. The Russian armies were led by generals who directed the battles. The other warring countries employed similar chains of command.

Hat flaps could be pulled down to keep out the cold

Jerkin could be made of goat- or sheepskin

Ammunition pouch

THE BRITISH ARMY
At the start of war, the British army contained 247,432 regulars and 218,280 reservists. Soldiers wore a khaki uniform consisting of a single-breasted tunic with a folding collar, pants, puttees or leggings worn to protect the shins, and ankle boots. In the winter, soldiers were issued with additional items such as jerkins. Many wore knitted scarves and balaclavas sent from home.

Woolen puttees wrapped around shins

British soldier

Lee Enfield rifle No. 1 MkIII

Thick boots to protect feet

EMPIRE TROOPS
The British and French armies included large numbers of recruits from their colonial possessions in Africa, Asia, the Pacific, and the Caribbean. In addition, the British dominions of Australia, New Zealand, Canada, and South Africa sent their own armies to take part in the conflict. Many of these troops had never left their home countries before. These Annamites (Indo-Chinese), above, from French Indo-China were stationed with the French army at Salonika, Greece, in 1916. They wore their own uniforms rather than those of the French army.

EASTERN ALLIES
In Eastern Europe, Germany faced the vast Russian army, as well as smaller armies from Serbia and Montenegro. In the Far East, German colonies in China and the Pacific Ocean were invaded by Japan. These illustrations come from a poster showing Germany's enemies.

Russia

France

Britain

Belgium

Field tunic
(Waffenrock)

Steel helmets
were issued
in 1916

Tent cloth

Cartridge
pouch

Mauser rifle

Stick grenade

Gas
mask

German
soldier

French infantrymen photographed in 1918

WESTERN ALLIES
In Western Europe, Britain,
France, and Belgium were
allied against Germany.
The British and French
armies were large, but
the Belgian army was
small and inexperienced.
These illustrations come
from a German poster
identifying the enemy.

THE FRENCH ARMY
The French army was one
of the largest in Europe.
Including reservists and
colonial troops, the French
army totaled 3,680,000
trained men at the
outbreak of war.

French
infantryman,
known as *le poilu*

Water bottle

Haversack with
personal items

Lebel rifle

THE GERMAN ARMY
The German army
was the strongest in
Europe because it had
been preparing for
war. At the outbreak
of hostilities, it
consisted of 840,000
men. All men under
the age of 45 were
trained for military
service and belonged
to the reserve army.
On calling up the
reserves, the German
army could expand to
over four million
trained men.

Russia

Serbia

Montenegro

Japan

Joining up

WAR LEADER
British Prime Minister Herbert Asquith was caricatured as "the last of the Romans" and replaced by David Lloyd George in December 1916.

At the outbreak of war, every European country but one had a large standing army of conscripted troops ready to fight. The exception was Britain, which had a small army made up of volunteers. On August 6, 1914, the Secretary of War, Lord Kitchener, asked for 100,000 new recruits. Whole streets and villages of patriotic men lined up to enlist. Most thought they would be home by Christmas. By the end of 1915, 2,446,719 men had volunteered, but more were needed to fill the depleted ranks of soldiers. In January 1916, conscription was introduced for all single men aged 18–41.

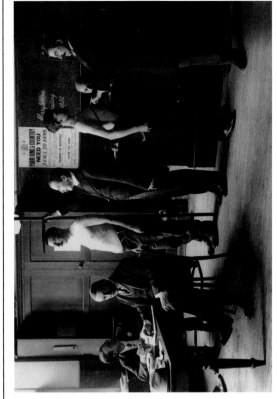

THE TEST
Every British recruit had to undergo a medical test to make sure he was fit to fight. Large numbers failed this test, because of poor eyesight, chest complaints, or general poor health. Others were refused because they were under 19, although many lied about their age. Once he passed the test, the recruit took the oath of loyalty to the king and was then accepted into the army.

"YOUR COUNTRY NEEDS YOU"
A portrait of the British War Minister, General Kitchener, was used as a recruiting poster. By the time it appeared in late September 1914, however, most potential recruits had already volunteered.

Small box respirator gas mask

Haversack contained the filter of the small box respirator

Pouch contained three clips, which each held five bullets

Two sets of five ammunition pouches on belt

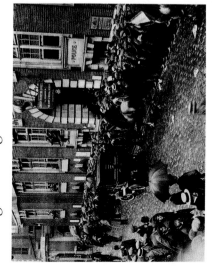

LINE UP HERE FOR KING AND COUNTRY
At the outbreak of war, long lines formed at recruiting offices around the country. Men from the same area or industry grouped together to form the famous Pals battalions, so they could fight together. By mid-September, half a million men had volunteered to fight.

Tin containing tea and stock cubes

Linen bag to store iron ration

Bully beef

Crackers

BISCUITS

RATIONS

Each soldier was given an "iron ration," consisting of hard crackers, corned beef, and a tin containing tea and stock cubes. Daily rations could include bread, hard crackers, "bully" meat, canned stew, canned pork and beans, sugar, tea, canned plum and apple jam, and canned butter. Ration parties carried the food to the front line in sandbags.

On les aura !

2ᴱ EMPRUNT DE
LA DÉFENSE NATIONALE *Souscrivez*

Haversack used for soldier's kit when in the trenches

Bayonet

Entrenching tool handle

Carry-all

Razor case

Boot laces

Water bottle

Knife

Straight razor

Soldier's small kit

Shaving brush

Fork

Spoon

Button stick

THE BASIC GEAR

A British soldier carried enough basic equipment to fight and to survive in the trenches. Along with his rifle and bayonet, he carried supplies of ammunition in pouches on his belt and an entrenching tool to dig a shallow hole to take cover in. By 1917, every soldier also carried a respirator in case of gas attacks. His survival gear included cutlery, washing kit, and spare clothes. When he went into battle, he transferred the most needed items out of his pack into a smaller haversack.

PAYING FOR THE TROOPS

The cost of raising and supplying vast armies meant each country had to raise taxes. Banks and private investors were asked to lend money to their government in the form of war loans. This famous French poster exhorts patriots to support the government's second national defense loan with the words "On les aura!" (We'll get them!).

EMPIRE TROOPS

When war was declared, thousands of men volunteered from across the British Empire. Existing regiments, such as these Bengal Lancers, were augmented by new recruits. Indian troops served with distinction on the Western Front, in German East Africa, and in the Middle East.

Conscientious objectors

Some people who refused to join up were given white feathers as a sign of cowardice. Certain religious groups objected to the war, since they believed it was wrong to kill, and some Socialists objected to fighting fellow workers. Both groups were known as conscientious objectors. Some objectors served in noncombatant units, such as medical services.

Life in the trenches

DAYTIME IN THE TRENCHES alternated between short periods of intense fear, when the enemy fired, and longer periods of boredom. Most of the work was done at night when patrols were sent out to observe and raid enemy trenches, and to repair their own front-line parapets and other defenses. Dawn and dusk were the most likely times for an enemy attack, so all the troops "stood to," that is manned the fire bays, at these times. The days were usually quiet, so the men tried to catch up on sleep while sentries watched the enemy trenches. Many soldiers used this time to write home or keep a diary of events. There were no set mealtimes on the front line, and soldiers ate as and when transportation was available to bring food to the front by carrying parties. To relieve the boredom, soldiers spent one week to 10 days in the front line, then moved into the reserve lines, and finally went to a rear area to rest. Here, they were given a bath and freshly laundered clothes before returning to the trenches.

A LITTLE SHELTER
The trenches were usually very narrow and often exposed to the weather. The Canadian soldiers in this trench have built a makeshift canopy to shelter under. The sides are made of sandbags piled on top of each other.

Soldier removing mud from ammunition pouch with a piece of cloth

A RELAXING READ?
This re-creation from London's Imperial War Museum shows a soldier reading. While there was plenty of time for the soldiers to read during the day, they were often interrupted by rats scurrying past their feet and itching lice in their clothes.

NEAT AND CLEAN
The cleaning of gear and the waterproofing of boots was as much a part of life in the trenches as it was in the barracks back home. These Belgian soldiers cleaning their rifles knew that such tasks were essential to maintaining combat efficiency.

OFFICERS' DUGOUT
This re-creation in London's Imperial War Museum of an officers' dugout on the Somme in the fall of 1916 shows the cramped conditions people endured in the trenches. The officer on the telephone is calling in artillery support for an imminent trench raid, while his weary comrade is asleep behind him on a camp bed. Official notices, photographs, and postcards from home are pinned around the walls.

The Menin Road (1918) by Paul Nash

French author Henri Barbusse (1873–1935) wrote of life in the trenches, denouncing the war in his novel *Le Feu (Under Fire)* of 1916.

Poem and self-portrait by British poet and artist Isaac Rosenberg (1890–1918)

Artists and poets

Some soldiers used their spare time in the trenches to write poems or make sketches. A huge number wrote long letters home, or kept a diary. After the war, many of these writings were published. Literary records of trench life made fascinating and shocking reading. In 1916, the British government began to send official war artists, such as Paul Nash (1889–1946), to the front to record the war in paint.

Paints and brushes belonging to British war artist Paul Nash

CAVE MEN
Ordinary soldiers—such as these members of the British Border Regiment at Thiepval Wood on the Somme in 1916—spent their time off duty in "funk holes," holes carved out of the side of the trench, or under waterproof sheets. Unlike the Germans, the British did not intend to stay in the trenches too long, so did not want the soldiers to make themselves comfortable.

TRENCH CUISINE
These French officers are dining well in a reserve trench in a quiet area. Others were less fortunate, enduring canned food or mass-produced meals cooked and brought up from behind the lines and reheated in the trench.

Soldiers served alongside a regiment of rats and lice

Ready to fight

IT IS EASY TO imagine that most of the action on the Western Front took place when soldiers left their trenches and fought each other in open ground, or no-man's-land, between the two opposing front lines. In reality, such events were far rarer than the constant battle between soldiers in their facing lines of trenches. Both armies took every opportunity to take shots at anyone foolish or unfortunate enough to be visible to the other side. Even soldiers trying to rescue wounded comrades from no-man's-land or retrieve bodies caught on the barbed-wire fences were considered fair targets. Raiding parties from one front line to the other added to the danger. This relentless war of attrition kept every soldier on full alert, and meant that a watch had to be kept on the enemy lines every hour of the day.

PREPARE TO FIRE
These German troops on the Marne in 1914 are firing through specially built gun holes. This enabled them to view and fire at the enemy without putting their heads above the parapet and exposing themselves to enemy fire. Later on in the war, sandbags replaced the dirt ramparts. On their backs, the troops carry leather knapsacks with rolled-up greatcoats and tent cloths on top.

IN CLOSE QUARTERS
Soldiers were armed with a range of close-combat weapons when they went on raiding parties in case they needed to kill an enemy. The enemy could be killed silently so that the raiding soldiers did not draw attention to themselves. The weapons were rarely used.

WRITING HOME
Canon Cyril Lomax served in France from 1916 to 1917 as a chaplain to the 8th Battalion Durham Light Infantry. As a noncombatant, he had time to describe in illustrated letters home some of the horrors he encountered. The armies of both sides had chaplains and other clergy at the front.

French trench knife

German stick grenade

German club

German timed and fused ball grenade

British Mills bomb

WALKING WOUNDED

This re-creation in London's Imperial War Museum shows a wounded German prisoner being escorted by a medical orderly from the front line back through the trench system to a regimental aid station. Many, however, were not so fortunate. A soldier wounded in no-man's-land would be left until it was safe to bring him back to his trench, usually at nightfall. Many soldiers risked their lives to retrieve wounded comrades. Sadly, some soldiers died because they could not be reached soon enough.

REGIMENTAL AID STATION

Battalion medical officers, as shown in this re-creation from London's Imperial War Museum, worked through the heat of battle and bombardment to treat the flood of casualties as best they could. They dressed wounds, tried to relieve pain, and prepared the badly wounded for the uncomfortable journey out of the trenches to the field hospital.

Path of bullet

ALWAYS IN ACTION

This photograph of Bulgarian soldiers was taken in 1915. It shows that soldiers could never let their guard down while in a trench. A permanent lookout must be kept, and guns always primed and ready in case the enemy mounted a sudden attack. The soldiers had to eat in shifts to ensure their constant readiness for battle.

SAVED BY A BOOK

The soldier carrying this book was lucky. By the time the bullet had passed through the pages, its passage was slowed enough to minimize the injury it caused.

"The German that I shot was a fine looking man … I did feel sorry but it was my life or his"

BRITISH SOLDIER JACK SWEENEY, NOVEMBER 21, 1916

Communication and supplies

COMMUNICATING WITH and supplying front-line troops is the biggest problem faced by every army. On the Western Front, this problem was particularly acute because of the length of the front line and the large number of soldiers fighting along it. In mid-1917, for example, the British army required 500,000 shells a day, and million-shell days were not uncommon. To supply such vast and hungry armies, both sides devoted great attention to lines of communication. The main form of transportation remained the horse, but increasing use was made of mechanized vehicles. Germany made great use of railroads to move men and supplies to the front. Both sides set up elaborate supply systems to ensure that front-line troops never ran out of munitions or food. Front-line troops also kept in close touch with headquarters and other units by telephone and wireless.

FIELD TELEPHONE
Telephones were the main communication method between the front line and headquarters. They relayed voice and Morse code messages.

GETTING IN TOUCH
Teams of engineers—such as this German group—were trained to set up, maintain, and operate telephones in the field. This allowed closer and more regular contact between the front line and HQ than in previous wars.

British night signal

MISSILE MESSAGES
Enemy fire often cut telephone lines, so both sides used shells to carry written messages. Flares on the shells lit up to signal their arrival. Signal grenades and rockets were also widely used to convey prearranged messages to front-line troops.

Message rolled up in base

German message shell

French army pigeon handler's badge

Canvas top secured with ropes

LOAD NOT TO EXCEED 3 TONS

↑ WD

PIGEON MAIL
Carrier pigeons were often used to carry messages to and from the front line where telephone lines did not exist. In fact, the noise and confusion of the front meant that the birds easily became bewildered and flew off in the wrong direction. Germany used "war dogs" specially trained to carry messages in containers on their collars.

*Soldier hitching a
ride to the front on
a supply wagon*

*Supply trucks
heading for
the front*

TWO-WAY TRAFFIC
One of the main
problems on the Western
Front was the lack of good roads
to and from the front line. Quiet
country lanes suddenly became major
thoroughfares as columns of marching
men, supply trucks, munitions wagons, field
ambulances, and other vehicles forced their way
through. The traffic was frequently two-way, with
soldiers ready for combat marching to the front,
passing their exhausted and often wounded
comrades heading in the opposite direction.

*Wounded British
troops returning
from the trenches in
November 1916*

WHEEL POWER
Both sides used trucks and vans to ferry men
and supplies to the front line. This British
3-ton (3,050-kg) Wolseley transportation
truck was specially built for war service, but
other smaller trucks and vans were also used.

61729

Open driver's cab

British Wolseley 3-ton
(3,050-kg) transport truck

*Sides dropped down
for access*

FABULOUS BAKER GIRLS
Behind the lines, vast quantities of food were
produced every day to feed the soldiers at the
front. British kitchens, cafeterias, and bakeries,
such as this one in Dieppe, France, were often
staffed by members of the Women's Army
Auxiliary Corps (W.A.A.C.). The Corps was set up
in February 1917 to replace the men needed to
fight on the front line. Women also played a
major role as clerks, telephone operators, and
storekeepers, ensuring that the front line was
adequately supplied and serviced at all times.

Observation and patrol

GATHERING INTELLIGENCE ABOUT the enemy is of great importance during war, because that information can be used to mount a successful attack or repel an enemy advance. Interrogating prisoners was a very successful method of gathering information. Additionally, along the Western Front, both sides were ingenious in devising new methods to gather intelligence. Nighttime patrols probed the strengths and weaknesses of enemy lines. This was hazardous work, since it meant crossing rows of barbed-wire entanglements and perhaps disturbing an unexploded shell or attracting enemy gunfire. Observation turrets and periscopes were also used. Aircraft became increasingly popular since they could fly virtually unhindered over the enemy, observe their trenches and gun emplacements, and photograph the front line. This information could then be used to produce maps of the enemy lines.

Canvas wing over wooden frame

AERIAL RECONNAISSANCE
Both sides used aircraft to observe enemy positions on the Western Front. At first, Allied commanders were suspicious of this new method. But in September 1914, French Air Service pilots saw the advancing German armies change direction near Paris. This information enabled the Allies to stop the German advance into France at the Battle of the Marne. The BE2a, above and left, was strong, stable, and easy to fly, making it ideal for reconnaissance work. The craft's pilot, Lieutenant H. D. Harvey-Kelley was the first British pilot to land in France after the outbreak of war.

Leather case

Mother-of-pearl face to catch the light

Glass front

Twin-propeller engine

Twin-seater cockpit

Solid wheels

Royal Aircraft Factory
Blériot Experimental BE2a
used for reconnaissance and
light bombing

COMPASS BEARINGS
A night patrol could easily get lost in no-man's-land because obvious features of the landscape, such as lanes, woods, fields, and even hills had all been blown away. A reflective compass was, therefore, essential if the patrol was to navigate safely and get back alive to its own trench before daybreak.

Artificial tree was an exact replica of the real tree it replaced

Soldier rests on internal step-ladder while looking through camouflaged spy-hole

German stereoscopic periscope

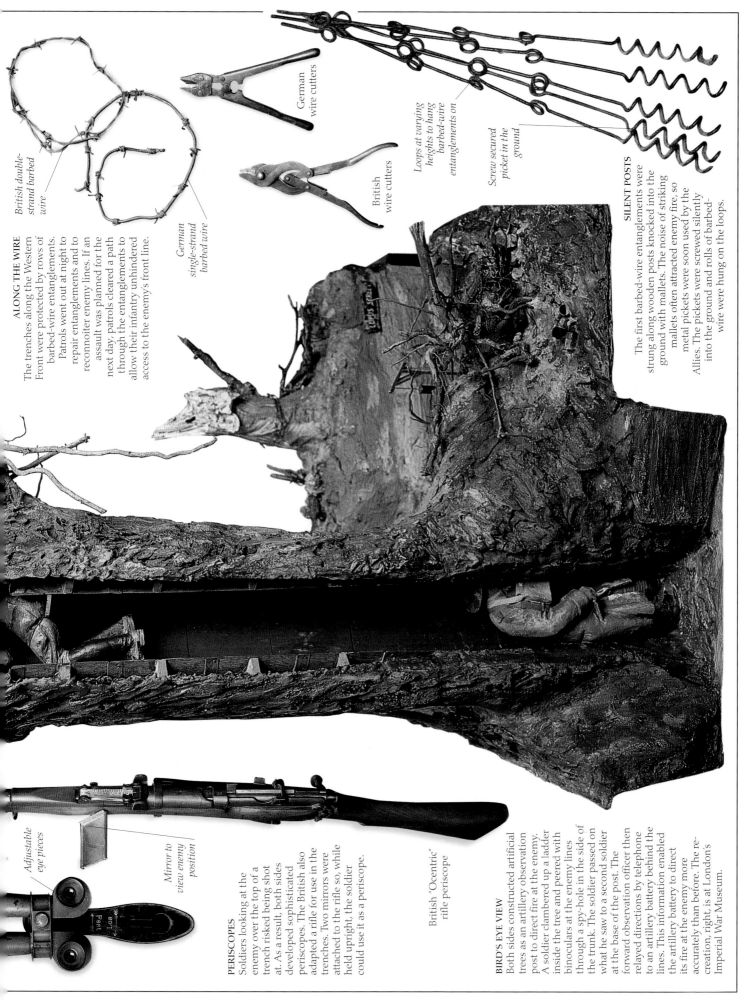

ALONG THE WIRE

The trenches along the Western Front were protected by rows of barbed-wire entanglements. Patrols went out at night to repair entanglements and to reconnoiter enemy lines. If an assault was planned for the next day, patrols cleared a path through the entanglements to allow their infantry unhindered access to the enemy's front line.

British double-strand barbed wire

German single-strand barbed wire

German wire cutters

British wire cutters

Loops at varying heights to hang barbed-wire entanglements on

Screw secured picket in the ground

SILENT POSTS

The first barbed-wire entanglements were strung along wooden posts knocked into the ground with mallets. The noise of striking mallets often attracted enemy fire, so metal pickets were soon used by the Allies. The pickets were screwed silently into the ground and rolls of barbed-wire were hung on the loops.

PERISCOPES

Soldiers looking at the enemy over the top of a trench risked being shot at. As a result, both sides developed sophisticated periscopes. The British also adapted a rifle for use in the trenches. Two mirrors were attached to the rifle so, while held upright, the soldier could use it as a periscope.

Adjustable eye pieces

Mirror to view enemy position

British "Ocentric" rifle periscope

BIRD'S EYE VIEW

Both sides constructed artificial trees as an artillery observation post to direct fire at the enemy. A soldier clambered up a ladder inside the tree and peered with binoculars at the enemy lines through a spy-hole in the side of the trunk. The soldier passed on what he saw to a second soldier at the base of the post. The forward observation officer then relayed directions by telephone to an artillery battery behind the lines. This information enabled the artillery battery to direct its fire at the enemy more accurately than before. The re-creation, right, is at London's Imperial War Museum.

SIGHT SAVER
In 1916–17 a chain-mail visor was added to the basic British helmet to protect the eyes. Visors were soon removed, since they were difficult to see through.

BEWARE!
Soldiers at the front needed constant reminders to keep their heads down since they were so used to shells flying past. Warning signs were common.

Bombardment

ARTILLERY DOMINATED the battlefields of World War I. A well-aimed bombardment could destroy enemy trenches and knock out artillery batteries and communication lines. It could also help break up an infantry attack. But as defensive positions strengthened, artillery bombardments became longer and more intense. New tactics were required to break down enemy lines. The most effective was the creeping barrage, which rained down a moving curtain of heavy and insistent fire just ahead of attacking infantry.

Helmet

Visor for extra protection

GERMAN ARMOR
In January 1916 the German army replaced its distinctive spiked *Pickelhaube* helmet with a rounded steel helmet. Body armor was first issued in 1916 to machine gunners.

Breastplate

Articulated plates to cover lower body

HIDING THE GUN
Two main types of artillery were used during the war— light field artillery, pulled by horses, and heavier guns, such as howitzers, moved by tractor and set up on reinforced beds. Once in place, artillery pieces were camouflaged to conceal them from the enemy.

British 8-in (20-cm) Mark V howitzer

SHELL POWER
The huge number of shells needed to maintain a constant artillery barrage against the enemy can be seen in this photograph of a British shell dump behind the Western Front.

LOADING A HOWITZER
Large pieces of artillery required a team of experienced gunners to load and fire them. This British 15-in (38-cm) howitzer was used on the Menin Road near Ypres, Belgium, in October 1917. The huge shell on the left of the picture is too large and heavy to lift, so it is being winched into position.

EXPLOSION!
The devasting impact of artillery fire can be seen in this dramatic picture of a British tank hit by a shell and bursting into flames. To its right, another tank breaks through the barbed wire. It was unusual for moving targets such as tanks to be hit, and most artillery fire was used to soften up the enemy lines before an attack.

British 13-pounder
(5.9-kg) high-
explosive shell

French
3-in
(75-mm)
shrapnel
shell

*Fired from
a howitzer*

British 4.5-in
(11.4-cm) high-
explosive shell

German 6-in (15-cm)
shrapnel shell

CLASSIFYING SHELLS
Shells were classified by weight or diameter. High-explosive shells exploded on impact. Antipersonnel shrapnel shells exploded in flight and were designed to kill or maim.

Over the top

ONCE THE ARTILLERY bombardment had pounded the enemy's defenses, the infantry climbed out of their trenches and advanced toward enemy lines. The advance was very dangerous. Artillery bombardments rarely knocked out every enemy defense. Often, many gun emplacements and barbed-wire fences were still intact. Gaps in the defensive line were filled by highly mobile machine-gunners. Against them, a soldier armed with only a rifle and bayonet and laden with heavy equipment was an easy target. On the first day of the Battle of the Somme in July 1916, German machine-gun fire accounted for two British soldiers killed or injured along each yard (meter) of the 16-mile (28-km) front.

LEAVING THE TRENCH
The most frightening moment for a soldier was scrambling up a ladder out of his trench and into no-man's-land. Few men knew the horrors that awaited them.

Steel water jacket to cool gun barrel

Disk is part of the flash hider assembly, making the gun harder to spot

German MG '08 Maxim machine gun

Trench mounting

IN ACTION
This German machine-gun crew is protecting the flank (side) of an advancing infantry troop on the Western Front. The reliability and firepower of machine guns made them effective weapons. Also, their small size and maneuverability made them difficult for the enemy to destroy.

QUICK FIRING
Machine guns fired up to 600 bullets a minute. Ammunition was fitted into a fabric or metal-link belt, or in a metal tray fed into the gun automatically. The gun barrel was surrounded with a cold-water jacket to cool it.

British .303-in (7.7-mm) Maxim Mark 3 medium machine gun

Water-cooled barrel

Tripod mounting

FUTILE ATTACK

The Battle of the Somme lasted from July 1, 1916, until November 18, when snowstorms and rain brought the attack to a muddy halt. The Allies captured about 48 sq miles (125 sq km) of land, but failed to break through the German lines, reducing much of the area to a desolate wasteland. The Germans had been on the Somme since 1914, so knew the terrain well. The British belonged to Kitchener's new army. Young and inexperienced, this was the first battle many of them had fought in.

"The sunken road ... (was) ... filled with pieces of uniform, weapons, and dead bodies."

LIEUTENANT ERNST JUNGER,
GERMAN SOLDIER,
THE SOMME, 1916

First day on the Somme

The Allies planned to break through the German lines north of the Somme River, France, in 1916. On June 24, the British began a six-day artillery bombardment on German lines, but the Germans retreated into deep bunkers and were largely unharmed. As the British infantry advanced at 7:30 a.m. on July 1, German machine gunners emerged from their bunkers and opened fire. Believing the artillery bombardment had destroyed German lines, the infantry marched in long, slow waves toward the enemy, who literally mowed them down.

Below: Soldiers of the 103rd (Tyneside Irish) Brigade attack La Boisselle on the first day of the Somme

TENDING THE WOUNDED

The cramped conditions in a trench can be seen in this picture of an army medical officer tending a wounded soldier at Thiepval near the Somme in September 1916. Movement along a trench was often difficult and slow.

Casualty

No one knows how many soldiers were wounded in the war, but a possible figure is 21 million. Caring for casualties was a major military operation. They were first treated at regimental aid stations in the trenches. Then, they were taken to casualty clearing stations behind the front line. Here, they received proper medical attention and basic surgery, if required, before being transported to base hospitals still farther from the front. Soldiers with severe injuries went home to recover in convalescent hospitals. Over 78 percent of British soldiers on the Western Front returned to active service. Sickness was a major cause of casualty—in some areas, over 50 percent of deaths were due to disease.

LUCKY MAN
Despite a splinter from a shell piercing his helmet, this soldier escaped with only a minor head wound. Many soldiers were not so fortunate, receiving severe injuries that stayed with them for life—if they survived at all.

Inventory listing contents and where to find them in the pouch

Bottles of liquid antiseptics and pain-killers

THE GERMAN KIT
German *Sanitätsmannschaften* (medical orderlies) carried two first-aid pouches on their belts. The pouch on the right (above) contained basic antiseptics, pain-killers, and other treatments, while the pouch on the left contained dressings and triangular bandages.

TRENCH AID
Injured soldiers had their wounds dressed by medical orderlies in the trenches where they fell. They were then transferred to the regimental aid station, where their injuries could be assessed.

Strip of lace curtain

RECYCLED BANDAGES
Following the naval blockade by Britain, Germany ran out of cotton and linen. Wood fiber, paper, and lace curtains were used to make bandages instead.

German bandages

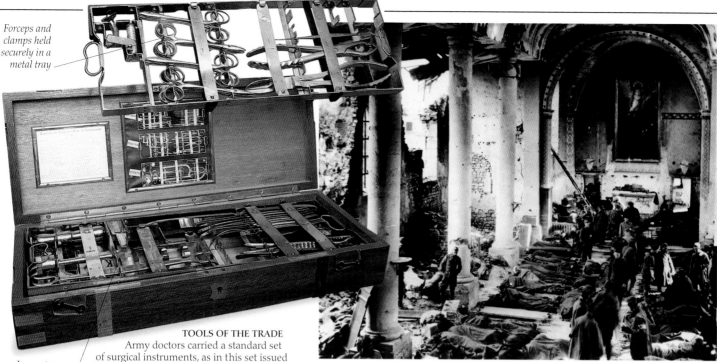

Forceps and clamps held securely in a metal tray

Lower tray contains saws and knives for amputation

TOOLS OF THE TRADE
Army doctors carried a standard set of surgical instruments, as in this set issued by the Indian army. Their skills were in great demand, as they faced a wide variety of injuries from bullets and shell fragments that required immediate attention.

THE FIELD HOSPITAL
Farmhouses, ruined factories, and even bombed-out churches, such as this one in Meuse, France, were used as casualty clearinghouses to treat the wounded. Care was basic, and many were left to help themselves.

Shellshock

Shellshock is the collective name that was used to describe concussion, emotional shock, nervous exhaustion, and other similar ailments. Shellshock was not identified before World War I, but trench warfare was so horrific that large numbers of soldiers developed symptoms. Most of them eventually recovered, but some suffered nightmares and other effects for the rest of their lives. The condition caused great controversy, and in 1922 the British War Office Committee announced that shellshock did not exist and was a collection of already known illnesses.

A medical orderly helps a wounded soldier away from the trenches

Bunks for the injured to lie on

AMBULANCE
The British Royal Army Medical Corps, like its German counterpart, had a fleet of field ambulances to carry the wounded to the hospital. Many of these ambulances were staffed by volunteers, often women, and those from noncombatant countries such as the US.

Red Cross symbol to signify non-combatant status of the ambulance

Women at war

WHEN THE MEN went off to fight, the women were called upon to take their place. Many women already worked, but their role was restricted to domestic labor, nursing, teaching, agricultural work on small family farms, and a few other jobs considered suitable for women. Now they went to work in factories, drove trucks and ambulances, and did almost everything that only men had done before. Many working women left their low-paid, low-status jobs for higher-paid work in munitions and other industries, achieving a new status in the eyes of society. Such gains, however, were short-lived, since most women returned to the home when the war ended.

FRONT-LINE ADVENTURE
For some women, the war was a big adventure. English nurse Elsie Knocker (above) went to Belgium in 1914 where she was joined by Scottish Mairi Chisholm. The women set up a dressing station at Pervyse, Belgium, and dressed the wounded until both were gassed in 1918. They were almost the only women on the front line. The two became known as the Women of Pervyse and were awarded the Order of Leopold by Belgian King Albert, and the British Military Medal. Elsie later married a Belgian officer, Baron de T'Sercles.

ARMY LAUNDRY
Traditional prewar women's work, such as working in a laundry or bakery, continued during the war on a much larger scale. The French women employed at this British Army laundry at Prevent, France, in 1918 were washing and cleaning the dirty clothes of many thousands of soldiers every day.

QUEEN MARY'S AUXILIARY
Few women actually fought in the war, but many were enlisted into auxiliary armies so that men could be released to fight on the front line. They drove trucks, repaired engines, and did much of the necessary administration and supply work. In Britain, many women joined The Women's (later Queen Mary's) Army Auxiliary Corps, whose recruiting poster featured a khaki-clad woman (left) with the words "The girl behind the man behind the gun." The women remained civilians, despite their military work.

WOMEN'S LAND ARMY

The war required a huge increase in food production at home as both sides tried to restrict the enemy's imports of food from abroad. In Britain, 113,000 women joined the Women's Land Army, set up in February 1917 to provide a well-paid female workforce to run the farms. Many members of the Land Army, such as this group of healthy looking women, came from the middle and upper classes. They made a valuable contribution, but their numbers were insignificant compared with the millions of working-class women already employed on the land in the rest of Europe.

SUPPORT YOUR COUNTRY

Images of "ideal" women were used to gain support for a country's war effort. This Russian poster urges people to buy war bonds (fund-raising loans to the government) by linking Russian women to the love of the motherland.

RUSSIA'S AMAZONS

A number of Russian women joined the "Legion of Death" to fight for their country. The first battalion from Petrograd (St. Petersburg) distinguished itself by taking more than 100 German prisoners during a Russian retreat, although many of the women died in the battle.

WORKING IN POVERTY

The war brought increased status and wealth to many women but this was not the case everywhere. These Italian women worked in terrible conditions in a munitions factory. Many were very young and could not even afford shoes. This was common in factories across Italy, Germany, and Russia. The women worked long, hard hours but earned barely enough to feed their families. Strikes led by women were very common as a result.

Letters to men at the front describing events at home

Family photographs

MEMENTOS FROM HOME

Women kept in contact with their absent husbands, brothers, and sons by writing letters to them at the front. They also enclosed keepsakes, such as photographs or pressed flowers, to reassure the men that all was well in their absence and to remind them of home. Such letters and mementos did much to keep up the morale of homesick and often very frightened men.

Lace handkerchief

War in the air

DOGFIGHTS
Pilots engaged in dogfights with enemy aircraft above the Western Front. Guns were mounted on top of the craft, so pilots had to fly straight at the enemy to shoot.

WHEN WAR BROKE OUT in August 1914, the history of powered flight was barely 10 years old. Aircraft had fought briefly in the Italian-Turkish war of 1911, but early aircraft development had been almost entirely for civilian use. Some military leaders could not even see how aircraft could be used in war but they soon changed their minds. The first warplanes flew as reconnaissance craft, looking down on enemy lines or helping to direct artillery fire with great precision. Enemy pilots tried to shoot them down, leading to dogfights in the sky between highly skilled and immensely brave "aces." Specialized fighter planes, such as the Sopwith Camel and the German Fokkers, were soon produced by both sides, as were sturdier craft capable of carrying bombs to drop on enemy targets. By the end of the war, the role of military aircraft had changed from being a minor help to the ground forces into a major force in their own right.

Leather face mask

Leather balaclava

Antisplinter glass goggles

Turned-up collar to keep neck warm

Pouch to keep maps in

Coat of soft, supple leather

Sheepskin-lined leather gloves to protect against frostbite

SOPWITH CAMEL
The Sopwith F1 Camel first flew in battle in June 1917 and became the most successful Allied fighter in shooting down German aircraft. Pilots enjoyed flying the Camel because of its exceptional agility and ability to make sharp turns at high speed.

Wooden box-structure wings covered with canvas

26-ft 11-in (8.2-m) wingspan

Propeller to guide the bomb

BOMBS AWAY
The first bombs were literally dropped over the side of the aircraft by the pilot. Specialized bomber aircraft soon appeared, equipped with bombsights, bomb racks beneath the fuselage, and release systems operated by the pilot or another crew member.

Fins to stop the bomb from spinning on its descent

Perforated casing to help bomb catch fire on impact

DRESSED FOR THE AIR
Pilots flew in open cockpits, so they wore soft leather coats and balaclavas, sheepskin-lined fur boots, and sheepskin-lined leather gloves to keep out the cold. Later in the war, one-piece suits of waxed cotton lined with silk and fur became common.

Sheepskin boots

British 20-lb (9.1-kg) Marten Hale bomb, with 4½ lb (2 kg) of explosives

British Carcass incendiary bomb

Thick sole to give a good grip

Fokker DVII

GERMAN FIGHTER
The formidable German Fokker DVII appeared in April 1918. Although slower than the Sopwith Camel, it climbed rapidly, recovered quickly from a dive, and flew well at all altitudes.

Side cutaway to show internal steel-tubing framework

BMW engine

MANEUVERS
The art of aerial warfare was unknown to pilots at the start of the war and had to be learned from scratch. This British instruction poster shows the correct method of attacking a German fighter, although theory on the ground was no substitute for actual experience in the sky.

German aircraft holds a steady course

British fighter comes up from below and behind

Wooden struts

Symbol of British Royal Flying Corps, later the Royal Air Force

N6812

"You ask me to 'let the devils have it'… when I fight… I don't think them devils … I only scrap because it is my duty."

CAPTAIN ALBERT BALL, 1916

Barrel could fire 1-pound (453.6-g) shell

Rittmeister Manfred von Richthofen (Germany), center— 80 hits (1892–1918)

Pivot to change direction and angle of gun

Captain René Fonck (France)—75 hits (1894– 1953)

Captain Albert Ball (Britain)—44 hits (1896–1917)

AIR ACES
To qualify as an air "ace," a pilot had to bring down at least 10 enemy aircraft. Those who did became national heroes. Baron von Richthofen—the "Red Baron"—was the highest-scoring ace of the war, shooting down 80 Allied aircraft. The British ace, Captain Albert Ball, had more decorations for bravery than any other man of his age, including the Victoria Cross; he was only 20 when he was shot down and killed in 1917.

Captain Eddie Rickenbacker (US)—24 1/3 hits (1890–1973)

ANTIAIRCRAFT GUNS
The first antiaircraft guns, such as this British QF 1-pounder, were originally installed on ships to fire at torpedo boats. Once adapted for high-angle shooting, they became useful antiaircraft guns on land.

Zeppelin

In the spring of 1915, the first German airships appeared in Britain's night sky. The sight of these huge, slow-moving machines caused enormous panic—at any moment a hail of bombs could fall from the airship. Yet in reality, airships played little part in the war. The first airship was designed by the German Count Ferdinand von Zeppelin in 1900. Airships are often called zeppelins, but technically only those designed by him should bear the name. Early in the war, airships could fly higher than planes, so it was almost impossible to shoot them down. This made them useful for bombing raids. But soon, higher flying aircraft and the use of incendiary (fire-making) bullets brought these aerial bombers down to earth. By 1917, most German and British airships were restricted to reconnaissance work at sea.

Fuel tank   *Gondola*

INSIDE THE GONDOLA
The crew operated the airship from the gondola—a spacious cabin below the main airship. The gondola had open sides, so the crew had little protection from the weather.

BOMBS AWAY!
Crews in the first airships had to drop their bombs, such as this incendiary bomb, over the side of the gondola by hand. Later models had automatic release mechanisms.

German incendiary bomb dropped by Zeppelin LZ38 on London, May 31, 1915

GETTING BIGGER
This L3 German airship took part in the first airship raid on Britain on the night of January 19–20, 1915, causing 20 civilian casualties. Eyewitnesses were scared by its size, but by 1918 Germany was producing ships almost three times as big.

Stabilizer

Emblem of British
Royal Naval Air
Service

SEA SCOUT ZERO
The British SSZ (Sea Scout Zero) was first
introduced into service in 1916. It was a
nonrigid airship, meaning it had no internal
framework. Its light weight gave it an
impressive top speed of 45 mph (72 kph)
and it could stay airborne for 17 hours. Its
crew of three were employed mainly on
submarine patrol or on escort duty
for convoys.

Observer

Engine and
propeller to
provide power
and steer airship

The engine gantry was
linked to the gondola
by a rope ladder

Gantry

Float in case
airship
landed on sea

Lewis gunner

HIGH ABOVE THE SEAS
The British used airships
chiefly to patrol the seas
looking for German U-boats.
The machine gunner
protected the crew and ship
against an enemy fighter,
while other crew members
were on lookout. These two
crew members are perching
on a flimsy gantry mounted
to the side of the gondola
strung beneath the airship.

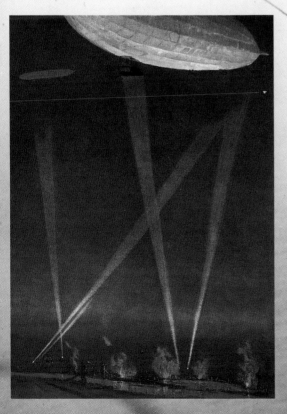

CAPITAL TARGET
The first German airship raid on London took
place on May 31, 1915, and was followed by a
more powerful attack on September 8. The
artist R. Schmidt from Hamburg recordecd one
such night raid. In total, there were 51 airship
attacks on British cities. They dropped 4,400 lb
(2,000 kg) of bombs, killing 557 people and
wounding 1,358.

War at sea

SINCE THE LAUNCH OF Britain's *Dreadnought* battleship in 1906, Britain, Germany, and other countries had engaged in a massive naval building program. Yet the war itself was fought largely on land and both sides avoided naval conflict. The British needed their fleet to keep the seas open for merchant ships bringing food and other supplies to Britain, as well as to prevent supplies from reaching Germany. Germany needed its fleet to protect itself against possible invasion. The only major sea battle—off Danish Jutland in the North Sea in 1916—was inconclusive. The main fight took place under the sea, as German U-boats waged a damaging war against Allied merchant and troop ships in an effort to force Britain out of the war.

"I WANT YOU"
When the US entered the war in April 1917, a poster showing an attractive woman in naval uniform (above) urged volunteers to enlist.

CONSTANT THREAT
This German propaganda poster, *The U-boats are out!*, shows the threat posed to Allied shipping by the German U-boat fleet.

LIFE INSIDE A U-BOAT
Conditions inside a U-boat were cramped and uncomfortable. Fumes and heat from the engine and poor ventilation made the air very stuffy. The crew had to navigate the craft through minefields, and avoid detection from reconnaissance aircraft, in order to attack enemy ships.

Floats for landing on water

LAND AND SEA
Seaplanes are able to take off and land on both water and ground. They were used for reconnaissance and bombing work. This version of the Short 184 was the first seaplane to sink an enemy ship with a torpedo.

Observation balloon

Gun

SUCCESS AND FAILURE
German U-boats operated both under the sea and on the surface. Here, the crew is opening fire with a deck cannon to stop an enemy steamer. German U-boats sank 5,554 Allied and neutral merchant ships as well as many warships. Their own losses, however, were also considerable. Out of a total fleet of 372 German U-boats, 178 were destroyed by Allied bombs or torpedoes.

CONFUSE AND SURVIVE

In 1917 the British Admiralty began to camouflage merchant ships with strange and garish designs. These gray, black, and blue geometric patterns distorted the silhouette of the ship and made it difficult for German U-boats to determine its course and thus aim torpedoes at it with any accuracy. More than 2,700 merchant ships and 400 convoy escorts were camouflaged in this way before the war ended.

DAZZLED

During the war, many artists contributed to their country's war effort, some in surprising ways. The modern British painter Edward Wadsworth supervised the application of "dazzle" camouflage to ships' hulls. He later painted a picture (above), *Dazzle ships in dry dock at Liverpool,* showing the finished result.

Medals awarded to Jack Cornwall

Victoria Cross (VC)

British War Medal

Victory Medal

BOY (1ST CLASS)

John Travers Cornwall was only 16 when he first saw action at the Battle of Jutland on May 31, 1916. He was a ship's boy (1st class) aboard HMS *Chester* and was mortally wounded early in the battle. While other crew members lay dead or injured, Cornwall stayed at his post until the end of the action. He died of his wounds on June 2 and was awarded the Victoria Cross posthumously.

THE BRITISH GRAND FLEET

The British Royal Navy was the biggest and most powerful in the world. It operated a policy known as the "two-power standard"—the combined might of the British fleet should be the equal of the two next strongest nations combined. Despite this superiority, the navy played a fairly minor role in the war compared with the army, keeping the seas free of German ships and escorting convoys of merchant ships to Britain.

Flight deck

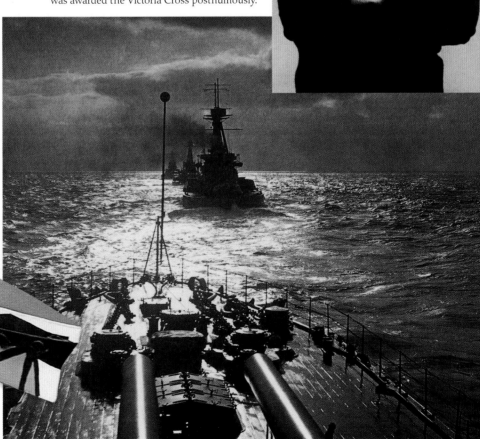

HMS *FURIOUS*

Aircraft carriers first saw service during World War I. On July 7, 1918, seven Sopwith Camels took off from the deck of HMS *Furious* to attack the zeppelin base at Tondern in northern Germany, destroying both sheds and the two Zeppelins inside.

Gallipoli

In EARLY 1915 the Allies decided to force through the strategic, but heavily fortified, Dardanelles straits and capture the Ottoman Turkish capital of Constantinople. Naval attacks on February 19 and March 18 both failed. On April 25, British, Australian, and New Zealand troops landed on the Gallipoli peninsula, while French troops staged a diversion to their south. In August, there was a second landing at Suvla Bay, also on the peninsula. Although the landings were a success, the casualty rate was high and the Allies were unable to move far from the beaches due to fierce Turkish resistance. As the months wore on, the death rate mounted. The Allies eventually withdrew in January 1916, leaving the Ottoman Empire still in control of the Dardanelles and still in the war.

GALLIPOLI PENINSULA
The Gallipoli peninsula lies to the north of the Dardanelles, a narrow waterway connecting the Aegean Sea to the Black Sea via the Sea of Marmara. Control of this waterway would have given Britain and France a direct sea route from the Mediterranean to the Black Sea and their ally, Russia. But both sides of the waterway were controlled by Germany's ally, the Ottoman Empire.

Privately purchased medical kit used by a British officer on the front line

Scissors   Scalpel   *Hypodermic needles*   Tweezers   *Pouch*

THE CASUALTY RATE
Despite the efforts of the medical staff, some of whom even carried portable surgical gear, the treatment and evacuation of casualties from Gallipoli was complicated by the enormous numbers of soldiers who were sick, as well as those who were wounded.

Jetty for boats carrying sick and wounded soldiers

THE SICK BEACH
Both sides had their food contaminated by flies carrying disease from the many corpses. Dysentery was endemic—in September 1915, 78 percent of the Anzac troops in the No. 1 Australian Stationary Hospital at Anzac Cove (above) were being treated for the disease.

GERMAN HELP
The Allies expected the Gallipoli peninsula to be lightly defended, but with the help of Germany, the Turks had built strong defensive positions. They dug trenches, erected barbed-wire fences, and built well-guarded artillery positions. Germany also equipped the Turks with modern pistols, rifles, and machine guns.

IMPROVISED GRENADES
The fighting at Gallipoli was often at very close range. Hand-thrown grenades were particularly effective in knocking out enemy positions. During a munitions shortage, Allied troops improvised by making grenades out of jam tin cans.

*Narrow beach unprotected
against Tukish fire*

*Turkish defenses look
down on beach*

KEMAL ATATURK

Born in 1881, Mustafa Kemal distinguished himself fighting for the Ottoman Turkish army in Libya in 1911 and against the Bulgarians in 1912–13. At Gallipoli, Kemal was appointed divisional commander, where he helped to strengthen the Ottoman Turkish defenses. Kemal then brilliantly led the 19th Division on the ridges above Anzac Cove, preventing the Allies from penetrating inland. After the war, Kemal led a revolt to prevent the dismemberment of Turkey. In 1923 he became the first president of the Turkish Republic, later gaining the name Atatürk (Father of the Turks).

ANZAC COVE

On April 25, the Australian and New Zealand Army Corps, known as the Anzacs, landed on the western coast of the Gallipoli peninsula. All hopes of swiftly capturing the peninsula were thwarted by the unyielding terrain. The beach was very narrow and the steep, sandy hills gave the men no cover. They were under constant fire from the well-hidden Ottoman Turks above. The beach is now known as Anzac Cove as a sign of remembrance.

Hyde Park Memorial, Sydney, Australia

*Sultan's Cypher with the year 1333
in the Muslim calendar, which is
1915 in the Western calendar*

FOR DISTINCTION

The Turkish Order of the Crescent was instituted on March 1, 1915, for distinguished service. It was awarded to German and Turkish soldiers who fought at Gallipoli.

ANZAC MEMORIAL

During the war, both Australia and New Zealand suffered large numbers of deaths in proportion to their small populations. Australia lost 60,000 men from a population of less than five million. New Zealand lost 17,000 from a population of one million. Of those, 11,100 died at Gallipoli. Today, Australia and New Zealand remember their war dead on Anzac Day, April 25.

WINTER EVACUATION

On December 7, 1915, the Allies decided to withdraw from Gallipoli. A flotilla of ships evacuated the troops and their supplies. Unlike the chaos and carnage of the previous six months, the withdrawals under the cover of darkness went without a hitch and not a single person was injured. British and Anzac forces withdrew from Anzac and Suvla on the night of December 18–19, with the rest of the British forces at Cape Helles following on January 8–9, 1916.

*Many soldiers were
suffering from frostbite*

*Large horse-
drawn gun*

*British soldiers evacuated by raft
from Suvla Bay, December 19, 1915*

Verdun

ON FEBRUARY 21, 1916, Germany launched a massive attack against Verdun, a fortified French city. Verdun lay close to the German border and controlled access into eastern France. After a huge, eight-hour artillery bombardment, the German infantry advanced. The French were caught by surprise and lost control of some of their main forts, but during the summer their resistance stiffened. By December, the Germans had been pushed back almost to where they started. The cost to both sides was enormous—over 400,000 French casualties and 336,831 German casualties. The German General Falkenhayn later claimed he had tried to bleed France to death. He did not succeed and, including losses at the Battle of the Somme, German casualties that year were 774,153.

BURNING WRECKAGE
On February 25, the ancient city of Verdun was evacuated. Many buildings were hit by the artillery bombardment, and even more destroyed by the fires that raged often for days. Firefighters did their best to control the blazes, but large numbers of houses had wooden frames and burned easily.

GENERAL PETAIN
General Henri-Philippe Pétain took command of the French forces of Verdun on February 25, the same day as the loss of Fort Douaumont. He organized an effective defense of the town and made sure the army was properly supplied. His rallying cry, "Ils ne passeront pas!" (They shall not pass!), did much to raise French morale.

Exposed concrete fort wall

Machine-gun post

FORT DOUAUMONT
Verdun was protected by three rings of fortifications. Fort Douaumont, in the outer ring, was the strongest of these forts. It was built of steel and concrete and surrounded by ramparts, ditches, and rolls of barbed wire. But although the fort itself was strong, it was defended by just 56 elderly reservists. The fort fell to the Germans on February 25.

Double-breasted greatcoat

Horizon-blue uniform

Haversack

LE POILU
The French slang for an infantry soldier was *le poilu*, or "hairy one." *Les poilus* bore the brunt of the German attack, enduring the muddy, cold, and wet conditions and suffering dreadful injuries from shellfire and poison gas.

Lebel rifle

Steel helmet

Thick boots with puttees wrapped around the legs

Background picture: Ruined Verdun cityscape, 1915

AT CLOSE QUARTERS

Fighting at Verdun was particularly fierce, as both sides repeatedly attacked and counterattacked the same forts and strategic areas around the city. Advancing attackers were assaulted by hails of machine-gun fire from the enemy within the forts. The open ground was so exposed that it was impossible to retrieve the dead, and corpses were left to rot in the ground. The forts were also riddled with underground tunnels, where both sides engaged in vicious hand-to-hand combat. Many dramatic movies have been made about the war, and this photograph comes from one such film.

"What a bloodbath, what horrid images, what a slaughter. I just cannot find the words to express my feelings. Hell cannot be this dreadful."

ALBERT JOUBAIRE
FRENCH SOLDIER, VERDUN, 1916

SURROUNDING VILLAGES

The village of Ornes was one of many French villages attacked and captured during the German advance on Verdun. The devastation was so great that this village, along with eight others, was not rebuilt after the war, but is still marked on maps as a sign of remembrance.

Laurel-leaf wreath

Oak-leaf wreath

Head of Marianne, symbol of France

LEGION D'HONNEUR

In recognition of the suffering experienced by Verdun's people, French president Raymond Poincaré awarded the city the *Légion d'Honneur*. The honor is usually presented to men and women, military and civilian, for bravery.

THE MUDDY INFERNO

The countryside around Verdun is wooded and hilly, with many streams running down to the Meuse River. Heavy rainfall and constant artillery bombardment turned this landscape into a desolate mudbath, where the bodies of the dead lay half-buried in shell craters and men were forced to eat and sleep within inches of their fallen comrades. This photograph shows the "Ravine de la mort," the Ravine of the Dead.

Gas attack

British "Hypo" helmet

On the afternoon of April 22, 1915, French-Algerian troops near the Belgian town of Ypres noticed a greenish-yellow cloud moving toward them from the German front. The cloud was chlorine gas. This was the first time poison gas had been used effectively in war. As it reached the Allied line, many soldiers panicked, for they had no protection against its choking effects. Over the next three years, both sides used gas—the Germans released 75,000 tons (68,000 metric tons), the British and French 56,000 tons (51,000 metric tons). The first gas clouds were released from canisters and blown by the wind toward the enemy, but this caused problems if the wind changed and blew the gas in the wrong direction. More effective were gas-filled shells, which could be targeted at enemy lines. In total, 1,200,000 soldiers were gassed, of whom 91,198 died terrible deaths.

EARLY WARNING
The first antigas masks were crude and often ineffectual, as these drawings from a British training school show. Basic goggles protected the eyes, while mouth-pads made of flannel or other absorbent materials were worn over the mouth. Chemicals soaked into the pads neutralized the gas.

British antigas goggles

Black veil respirator

Flannel respirator

Air tube

Chemical filter to neutralize gas

ALL-IN-ONE
By the middle of the war, both sides wore fully protective helmets, which consisted of face masks, goggles, and respirators. These protected the eyes, nose, and throat from the potentially lethal effects of gas.

British smallbox respirator

Gas alarm whistle

GASSED!
The full horror of being blinded by gas is caught in *Gassed*, a painting from real life by the American artist John Singer Sargent. Led by their sighted colleagues, the blinded soldiers are slowly shuffling toward a dressing station near Arras in northern France in August 1918.

Lachrymatory | Phosgene & Diphosgene | Diphosgene & Sneezing Oil | Diphosgene | Mustard Oil

GAS SHELLS

Gas shells contained liquid gas, which evaporated on impact. Gases caused a range of injuries depending on their type. Gases such as chlorine, diphosgene, and phosgene caused severe breathing difficulties while benzyl bromide caused the eyes to water. Dichlorethylsulfide burned and blistered the skin, caused temporary blindness and, if inhaled, flooded the lungs and led to death from pneumonia.

Glove shrunken by gas

Ordinary glove

HAND SHRUNK

When exposed to some kinds of gas, a glove like the one above will shrink to the size of the glove above, right. This is what happens to a person's lungs when exposed to the same gas.

UNDER ATTACK

The first effects of gas were felt on the face and in the eyes, but within seconds it entered the throat. Soldiers coughed and choked as the gas swirled around them. The long-term effects depended on the type of gas used—some soldiers died very quickly, others were blinded for life or suffered awful skin blisters, while some died a lingering death as their lungs collapsed and filled with liquid. The only protection was to wear combined goggles and respirator. Major Tracy Evert photographed these American soldiers in 1918. They are posing to illustrate the ill effects of forgetting their gas masks. The photograph was used when training new recruits.

German gas mask

Eyes not protected

Canvas-covered respirator

ANIMAL WELFARE

Every living creature was vulnerable to gas, including the many thousands of horses used by both sides to transport men, equipment, and supplies. Here, both German rider and horse have got their gas masks on, although the horse's eyes remain unprotected and vulnerable.

The Eastern Front

TANNENBERG, 1914
In August 1914, Russia's First and Second armies invaded East Prussia, Germany. The Russians did not disguise their messages in code, so the Germans knew what to expect. The Second Army was soon surrounded at Tannenberg and was forced to surrender on August 31, with the loss of 150,000 men and all of its artillery (above).

W HEN PEOPLE THINK today of World War I, they picture the fighting in the trenches along the Western Front. But on the other side of Europe, a very different war took place, between Germany and Austria-Hungary on one side and Russia on the other. This war was much more fluid, with great armies marching backward and forward across many hundreds of miles. Both the Austro-Hungarian and Russian armies were badly led and poorly equipped, and both suffered huge losses. In 1915 alone, the Russians lost two million men, of whom one million were taken prisoner. The German army, ably led by General Hindenburg, was far more effective. By the end of 1916, despite some Russian successes, the Germans were in full control of the entire Eastern Front. The Russians were greatly demoralized and this led, in part, to the Russian Revolution the following year, 1917.

MASURIAN LAKES, 1914
In September 1914, the Russian First Army had marched to the Masurian Lakes in East Prussia. It was in danger of being surrounded as the Second Army had been the previous month at Tannenberg. German troops dug trenches and other defenses (above) and attacked the Russians, who soon withdrew, sustaining more than 100,000 casualties. By the end of September, the Russian threat to Germany was over.

INITIAL SUCCESS
During 1914 the Russian army conquered Austria-Hungary's eastern province of Galicia, inflicting huge defeats on the Austro-Hungarian army. But, in 1915, German reinforcements (above) pushed the Russians back into their own country.

UNWILLING TO FIGHT
By the end of 1916, many Russian soldiers were refusing to fight. They were badly treated, ill-equipped, poorly led, and starving. They saw little reason to risk their lives in a war they did not believe in. Officers had to threaten their troops to make them fight, and mutinies were common, although many thousands simply deserted and went home.

Below: Russian troops marching to defend the newly captured city of Przemysl in Austrian Galicia

The Italian Front

On May 23, 1915, Italy joined the war on the side of the Allies and prepared to invade its hostile neighbor, Austria-Hungary. Fighting took place on two fronts—north and east. Italy fought against the Italian-speaking Trentino region of Austria-Hungary to the north, and along the Isonzo River to the east. The Italian army was ill-prepared and under-equipped for the war, and was unable to break through the Austrian defenses until its final success at the Battle of Vittorio-Veneto in October 1918.

THE ISONZO
The Isonzo River formed a natural boundary between the mountains of Austria-Hungary and the plains of northern Italy. Between June 1915 and August 1917, the two sides fought 11 inconclusive battles along the river before the Austrians, with German support, achieved a decisive victory at Caporetto in December 1917.

ITALIAN ALPINISTS
All but 20 miles (32 km) of the 400-mile (640-km) Italian frontier with Austria-Hungary lay in the Italian Alps. Both sides used trained alpine troops to fight in mountainous terrain. Every mountain peak became a potential observation post or gun emplacement.

War in the desert

FIGHTING DURING World War I was not restricted just to Europe. German colonies in Africa were overrun by French, British, and South African forces, while Germany's colonies in China and the Pacific were invaded by Japanese, British, Australian, and New Zealand forces. One of the major conflicts took place in the Middle East. Here, the Turkish Ottoman Empire controlled Mesopotamia (modern Iraq), Palestine, Syria, and Arabia. British and Indian troops invaded Mesopotamia in 1914 and finally captured Baghdad in 1917. Meanwhile, a large British force, under General Allenby, captured Palestine and, in the last weeks of the war, the Syrian capital of Damascus. In Arabia, Bedouin soldiers under the guidance of T. E. Lawrence rose in revolt against their Turkish rulers and waged a guerrilla campaign for an independent Arab state.

SPINE PAD
The British army was concerned that soldiers fighting in the desert might get heatstroke. They therefore issued spine pads to protect the soldiers' backs from the sun. The weight and discomfort of the pad would have done little to keep the body cool.

Arab flintlock pistol

Lawrence's rifle

Lawrence's initials

RETURN JOURNEY
British soldier T. E. Lawrence's rifle was one of the many British rifles captured by the Turks at Gallipoli in 1915. It was then given by the Turkish War Minister, Enver Pasha, to the Arab leader, Emir Feisal, who in turn presented it to Lawrence in December 1916.

LAWRENCE OF ARABIA
The British soldier T. E. Lawrence is a romantic, almost legendary figure known as Lawrence of Arabia. Lawrence first visited the Middle East in 1909, and learned to speak Arabic. In 1914 he became an army intelligence officer in Cairo, Egypt. Later, he worked as liaison officer to Emir Feisal, leader of the Arab revolt against Ottoman Turkish rule. Lawrence helped the Arabs to become an effective guerrilla force, blowing up railroad lines, attacking Turkish garrisons, and tying down an army many times their own size.

Signpost from a
crossroads in Jerusalem

FIGHTING IN PALESTINE

In early 1917, Britain opened a new front against
Ottoman Turkey. British troops invaded Palestine
and, after early failures, General Allenby captured
and entered Jerusalem on December 11, 1917 (left).
After a pause, fighting resumed in the fall of 1918.
British troops pushed north toward Damascus, while
an Arab army under Lawrence continued to attack
the Turks in the desert. Both armies entered
Damascus on October 1, 1918. Within a month,
Ottoman Turkey had surrendered.

*Swat made
of perforated,
flexible leather*

FLY SWAT
The British army made sure its
personnel were issued with
every necessity for desert
warfare, including fly swats!

Wire strap

Leather loop

Webbing strap

SAND SHOES
Walking across soft, shifting sand in
regular army boots was very tiring. These
British wire sand shoes were worn over
the boot and tied in place with webbing
straps. They helped spread the soldier's
weight, so he did not sink in the sand.

MARCH TO BAGHDAD
Turkish-held Mesopotamia was rich in
oil, which Britain needed to supply her
navy with fuel. In November 1914 Britain
sent troops to protect her interests in the
oil fields of Basra in Mesopotamia. The
commander, General Townshend, then
decided to advance up the Tigris River
toward Baghdad. But his men were
ill-prepared for a long campaign, and
in April 1916 their garrison at Kut
al-Amarah was forced to surrender to
Turkish troops, seen here crossing a
pontoon bridge in Baghdad. The British
finally captured Baghdad in March 1917.

German sign
celebrating the fall
of the Kut

Espionage

BOTH SIDES SUSPECTED the other of employing hundreds of spies to report on enemy intentions and capabilities. In fact, most espionage work consisted not of spying on enemy territory but of eavesdropping on enemy communications. Code-breaking or cryptography was very important as both sides sent and received coded messages by radio and telegraph. Cryptographers devised highly complex codes to ensure the safe transit of their own messages while using their skills to intercept and break coded enemy messages. Such skills enabled British intelligence to decipher the Zimmermann telegram from Berlin to Washington sent in January 1917, leading to the entry of the US into the war in April 1917.

Lightweight, but strong, string attaches parachute to bird

Corselet made of linen and padded to protect bird

PIGEON MAIL
Over 500,000 pigeons were used during the war to carry messages between intelligence agents and their home bases. The pigeons were dropped by parachute into occupied areas. Agents collected the pigeons at drop zones and looked after them until they had information to send home. When released, the birds flew home to their lofts with messages attached to their legs.

EDITH CAVELL
Edith Cavell was born in England and worked as a governess in Belgium in the early 1890s before training in England as a nurse. In 1907 she returned to Belgium to start a nursing school in Brussels (above). When the Germans occupied the city in August 1914 she decided to stay, accommodating up to 200 British soldiers who also found themselves behind enemy lines. The Germans arrested her and tried her for "conducting soldiers to the enemy." She was found guilty and executed by firing squad in October 1915. Cavell was not a spy, but her execution did provide a powerful propaganda weapon for the Allies.

IN MINIATURE
Pigeons could not carry much weight, so messages had to be written on small pieces of paper. This message, in German, is written on a standard "pigeon post" form used by the German army. Long messages could be photographed with a special camera that reduced them to the size of a microdot—that is 300 hundred times smaller than the original.

Front of button

Coded message on back of button

SECRET INK
Invisible ink was used to conceal messages written on paper. The invisible message could be read later when the paper was treated with a chemical to make the words visible.

German invisible ink and sponge

Invisible ink bottle

BUTTON MESSAGE
Coded messages could be written in the smallest and most unobtrusive of places. During the war, messages were stamped on to the back of buttons sewn on to coats or jackets.

POCKET CAMERA

Lens cap

Small cameras hidden in a pocket or disguised as a pocket watch were used to take secret photographs. This spy camera saw service in German East Africa (now Tanzania).

Camera lens

Shutter release

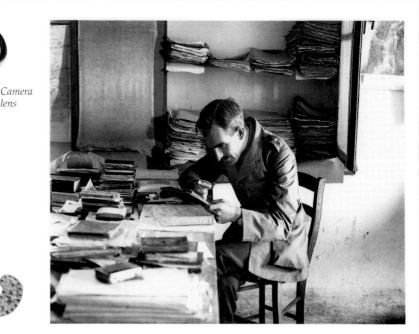

READING THE ENEMY

Army intelligence officers, such as this British soldier, played a vital role in examining and understanding captured enemy documents. Painstaking reading of every piece of information enabled the intelligence services to build up a reasonably complete picture about enemy preparations for an attack. They could also assess the state of civilian morale, and pass that information on to the military high command.

HIDDEN MESSAGES

Not every spy remained undetected. Two agents from the Netherlands sent to Portsmouth, England, to spy for Germany pretended to be cigar importers. They used their orders for imported Dutch cigars as codes for the ships they observed in Portsmouth Harbor. They were caught and executed in 1915.

Cigars slit open in search of hidden messages

AID TO ESCAPE

This tin, supposedly containing ox tongue, was sent to British Lieutenant Jack Shaw at the German Prisoner of War Camp Holzminden in 1918. It contained maps, wire cutters, and compasses to help Shaw arrange a mass escape from the camp.

Rolled-up map of France

Lead weights to make the tin the correct weight

Compass

MATA HARI

Dutch-born Margaretha Zelle was a famous dancer who used the stage-name Mata Hari. She had many high-ranking lovers, which enabled her to pass on any confidential information she acquired from them to the secret services. In 1914, while dancing in Paris, she was recruited by the French intelligence service. She went to Madrid, where she tried to win over a German diplomat. He double-crossed her with false information and on her return to France she was arrested, tried, and found guilty of being a German agent. She was executed by firing squad in October 1917.

Tank warfare

THE BRITISH-INVENTED tank was a major mechanical innovation of the war. British tanks first saw action in September 1916, but these early tanks were not very reliable. It was not until November 1917, at the Battle of Cambrai, that their full potential was realized. At Cambrai, the German defenses were so strong that an artillery bombardment would have destroyed the ground and made it impossible for the infantry to cross. Instead, fleets of tanks flattened barbed wire, crossed enemy trenches, and acted as shields for the advancing infantry. Tanks played a vital role in the Allied advances throughout 1918.

Stabilizer wheels

Carried crew of eight men

Total weight of 31 tons (28,450 kg)

Equipped with two 6-pounder guns and four machine guns

BRITISH MARK I HEAVY TANK
The first tank to fight in battle was the British Mark 1 tank. Forty-nine were ready to fight at the Battle of the Somme on 15 September 1916, but only 18 were reliable enough to take part in the battle itself.

Toughened leather skull cap

PROTECT AND SURVIVE
Leather helmets, faceguards, and chainmail mouthpieces were issued to British tank crews to protect their heads. The visors gave protection against particles of hot metal that flew off the inside of the hull when the tank was hit by a bullet.

Leather visor

Chainmail mouthpiece

German A7V tank

A7V TANK
The only German tank built during the war was the huge A7V, a 36-ton (33,500-kg) machine with six machine guns and a crew of 18. Only 20 A7Vs were constructed, and their appearance in spring 1918 was too late in the war to make any real impact.

British Mark V tank

INSIDE A TANK
Life inside a tank was very unpleasant. The tank was hot, fume-ridden, and badly ventilated, making the crew sick or even faint. The heat was sometimes so great in light tanks that it exploded the ammunition.

Rear entry hatch

Driver's entry hatch

Lid for driver's entry hatch

Driver's visor

T 9171

Iron caterpillar track

The driver and gunner were squashed in the front of the tank

Six men sat around the engine manning the guns

Six-cylinder engine

BRITISH MARK V TANK
The British Mark V tank first saw action in July 1918. It was equipped with two 6-pounder guns and four machine guns, and had a crew of eight. Its advanced system of gears and brakes allowed it to be driven and controlled by only one person.

Machine-gun port

DRIVING A TANK
The first British tanks were driven by two people, each controlling one track. They had a limited range of 25 miles (40 km) and their tracks broke regularly. Later tanks were driven by a single person and were more maneuverable and robust. However, they were still vulnerable to enemy shellfire, and often broke down, as here during the British assault on Arras in April 1917.

CROSSING THE TRENCHES
A tank could cross a narrow trench easily, but it could topple into a wide one. To solve this problem, the British equipped their tanks with circular metal bundles that could be dropped into a trench to form a bridge. Here, a line of Mark V tanks are moving in to attack German trenches during the fall of 1918.

The US enters the war

British medal suggesting the attack on SS *Lusitania* was planned

W HEN WAR broke out in Europe in August 1914, the US remained neutral. The country was deeply divided about the war, as many of its citizens had recently arrived from Europe and were strongly in favor of one side or the other. When German U-boats started to sink American ships, however, public opinion began to turn against Germany. In February 1917, Germany decided to attack all foreign shipping to try to reduce supplies to Britain. It also tried to divert US attention from Europe by encouraging its neighbor, Mexico, to invade. This action outraged the US government, and as more US ships were sunk, President Wilson declared war on Germany. This was now a world war.

SS *LUSITANIA*
On May 7, 1915, the passenger ship SS *Lusitania* was sunk off the coast of Ireland by German torpedoes because the ship was suspected of carrying munitions. The ship was bound from New York City to Liverpool, England. Three-quarters of the passengers drowned, including 128 US citizens. Their death did much to turn the US public against Germany and toward the Allies.

UNCLE SAM
The artist James Montgomery Flagg used himself as a model for Uncle Sam, a cartoon figure intended to represent every American. The portrait was based on Kitchener's similar pose for British recruiting posters (see page 14). Beneath his pointing finger were the words "I WANT YOU FOR THE US ARMY."

Ammunition clip

Belt

Water-bottle carrier

Field-dressing pouch

Ammunition pouch

Tube

Gas mask

Eyepiece

Field dressing

Filter box

Strap

Cup

Water bottle

Mess tin

Shaving kit

Shaving brush

Mess tin

Scabbard

Trench knife

Brass knuckle handle

PRESIDENT WILSON
Woodrow Wilson was a distinguished academic before he was elected president of the United States in 1912. As a war leader, he was principled and strong, but he was too idealistic and failed to get Congress to support the postwar peace treaty or the new League of Nations, which was designed to prevent another world war. In 1919 Wilson won the Nobel Peace Prize for his work in bringing peace to Europe.

INFANTRY EQUIPMENT
A US infantryman went to the Western Front prepared for every eventuality. Around his waist he wore a cartridge belt filled with ammunition, a water bottle, and a basic first aid kit. On his back he carried a heavy pack with a bayonet, an entrenching tool, a blanket, and his personal kit, which included a mess tin and essential toiletries.

GUN FIRE

The US First Army saw its first major action on September 12–16, 1918, at St. Mihiel, south of Verdun, France, as part of a combined Allied attack against German lines. Here an artillery crew fires a 3-in (75-mm) field gun as a spent shell-case flies through the air.

FOR HEROISM

Instituted by Presidential Order in 1918, the Distinguished Service Cross was awarded for extreme heroism against an armed enemy.

Securing strap for pack contents

M1905 Springfield bayonet

Haversack

Entrenching tool

Blanket or greatcoat roll

Assembled kit, US Infantry Equipment

KEEPING IN TOUCH

Like their colleagues in other armies, many US soldiers had hardly left their home town or state before, and few had ever traveled abroad. Stationed in France, in a country where they could not speak the language, many became deeply homesick. They wrote often to their family and friends, and waited for letters, postcards, and food parcels in return.

Under enemy lines

Air tubes

TO THE RESCUE
A gas attack or a shell burst near a mine tunnel entrance could fill the mine with fumes, suffocating the men working inside. This German breathing apparatus was kept on standby for use by rescue parties.

For much of the war on the Western Front, the two sides faced each other in rows of heavily fortified trenches. These massive defenses were very difficult to overcome, so engineers found ways of undermining them. The British army recruited coal miners and "clay-kickers," who used to dig tunnels for London Underground. The Germans had their own miners. Both excavated tunnels and mines deep under enemy lines and packed them with explosives, ready to be detonated when an attack began. Countermines were also dug to cut into and destroy enemy mines before they could be finished. The opposing miners sometimes met and fought in underground battles. Vast mines were exploded by the British at the Battle of the Somme on July 1, 1916, but their most effective use was under Messines Ridge at the start of the Battle of Passchendaele.

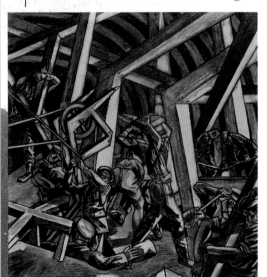

SAPPERS AT WORK
British artist David Bomberg's painting shows members of the Royal Engineers, known as "sappers," digging and reinforcing an underground trench. Sappers ensured that trenches and tunnels were well constructed and did not collapse.

Headpiece

Straps to hold mouthpiece in place

Nose clip

Air tube

Breathing bag was carried on chest

Air from oxygen cylinders carried on the back entered the breathing bag through this valve

OXYGEN RELIEF
This British breathing apparatus is similar to the German equipment on the left. Compressed oxygen contained in the breathing bags was released through the air tubes to help the miner breathe.

Background picture: One of many British mines explodes under German lines at the Battle of the Somme, July 1, 1916

"It is horrible. You often wish you were dead, there is no shelter, we are lying in water ... our clothes do not dry."

GERMAN SOLDIER, PASSCHENDAELE, 1917

WATERLOGGED
The water table around Ypres was very high, so the trenches were built above ground by banking up dirt and sandbags. Even so, the trenches were constantly flooded. Pumping out mines and trenches, as these Australian tunnelers are doing at Hooge, Belgium, in September 1917, was an essential, never-ending task.

Passchendaele

During 1917, the British planned a massive attack against the German front line around Ypres, Belgium. They aimed to break into Belgium and capture the channel ports, stopping the German submarines from using them as a base to attack British shipping. The Battle of Messines began on June 7, 1917. After a huge artillery bombardment, 19 mines packed with 1 million tons of explosive blew up simultaneously under the German lines on Messines Ridge. The noise could be heard in London 140 miles (220 km) away. The ridge was soon captured, but the British failed to take quick advantage. Heavy rainfall in August and October turned the battlefield into a muddy marshland. The village and ridge of Passchendaele were eventually captured on November 10, 1917, only to be lost again the following March. In the summer of 1918, the Allies recaptured and kept the ground.

MUDDY QUAGMIRE
Heavy rainfall and constant shelling at Passchendaele created a deadly mudbath. Many injured men died as they were unable to lift themselves clear of the cloying mud. Stretcher bearers were barely able to carry the wounded to dressing stations. The British poet Siegfried Sassoon wrote that "I died in hell—(They called it Passchendaele)."

Below: British troops moving forward over shell-torn ground during the Battle of Passchendaele.

NEW LEADER
In 1917, Vladimir Lenin, the leader of the Bolshevik (Communist) Party, became the new ruler of Russia. He was opposed to the war, and ordered an immediate cease-fire when he came to power.

German and Russian troops celebrating the cease-fire on the Eastern Front, 1917

Russia pulls out

The Russian government became increasingly unpopular as the war progressed. The army was demoralized by constant defeats, and by early 1917, there was large-scale fraternization with German troops along the Eastern Front. In February 1917, a revolution overthrew the czar, but the new government continued the war. A second revolution in October brought the Bolshevik Party to power. A cease-fire was agreed with Germany, and in March 1918 Russia signed the Treaty of Brest-Litovsk and withdrew from the war.

THE LUDENDORFF OFFENSIVE
On March 21, 1918, General Ludendorff launched a huge attack on the Western Front. He hoped to defeat Britain and France before US reinforcements could arrive. The attack took the Allies by surprise and Germany advanced by almost 40 miles (64 km) by July, but at the heavy cost of 500,000 casualties.

IN EARLY 1918, the war looked to be t in favor of Germany and her allies. Ru withdrawn from the war, enabling Germany to concentrate her effort the Western Front, and US troops yet to arrive in France in any grea numbers. A vast offensive in Mar brought German troops to within (40 miles) of Paris. But behind th Germany was far from strong. Th Allied blockade of German ports that the country was short of vita supplies. The railway network wa collapsing through lack of mainte and food was short. Strikes and ev mutinies became common. Elsew Ottoman Turkey and Bulgaria coll in the face of Allied attacks, while Italians scored a decisive victory a Austria-Hungary. By early Novem Germany stood alone. On 7 Nov a German delegation crossed the line to discuss peace terms with t Allies. The war was almost over.

Frenc durin

8 January US President Wilson issues 14 Points for Peace
3 March Treaty of Brest-Litovsk—Russia leaves the war
March 21 Vast German Ludendorff

offensive on the Western Front
July 15 Last German offensive launched on Western Front
July 18 French counterattack begins on the Marne

August 8 British launc near Amiens
September 12 Americ offensive at St. Mihiel
September 14 Allies a

BATTLE OF THE MARNE

On July 18, 1918, French and US forces, led by General Foch, counterattacked against the German advance on the Marne River, east of Paris. They stopped the German offensive in its tracks and began to push the Germans back eastward. By August 6, the Germans had lost 168,000 men, many buried where they fell on the battlefields (left). The tide of battle had at last turned decisively in favor of the Allied armies.

French soldiers identifying German dead before burial

CROSSING THE LINE

On August 8, 1918, a massive British offensive began near Amiens. The German army was increasingly short of men and vital supplies, including food, so gave little resistance. The Allied troops continued to push forward toward the heavily fortified Hindenburg Line, which had been built by the Germans as a fall-back defensive position. On September 29, the British 46th North Midland Division captured the bridge at Riqueval, over the St. Quentin Canal. They posed for a celebratory photograph, because they had broken the Line at last.

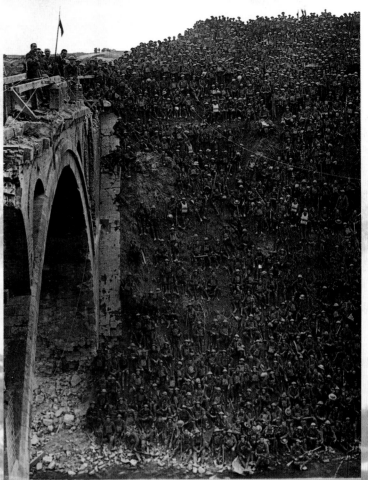

Many French children did not remember life before the German occupation of their towns and cities

Background picture: German troops advancing at the Somme, April 1918

French children march alongside the Allied army

THE LAST DAYS

By October 5, the Allied armies had breached the entire Hindenburg Line and were crossing open country. Both sides suffered great casualties as the German army was pushed steadily eastward. The British and French recaptured towns and cities lost in 1914, including Lille (left), and by early November 1918 they recaptured Mons, where they had fired the first shots of the war in August 1914. By now, the German retreat was turning into a rout.

September 28 German commander Ludendorff advises the Kaiser to seek peace as army crumbles
October 1 British capture Ottoman Turkish-held Damascus

6 October German government starts to negotiate an armistice
October 21 Czechoslovakia declares its independence
October 24 Italian army begins

decisive battle of Vittorio-Veneto against Austria-Hungary
October 29 German fleet mutinies
October 30 Ottoman Turkey agrees to an armistice

November 4 Austria-Hungary agrees to an armistice
November 9 The Kaiser abdicates
November 11 Armistice between Germany and the Allies; war ends

Armistice and peace

CAR TALKS
On November 7, 1918, a German delegation headed by a government minister, Matthias Erzberger, crossed the front line to meet the Allied commander-in-chief, Marshal Foch, in his railroad car in the forest of Compiègne. At 5 a.m. on November 11, the two sides signed an armistice agreement to come into effect six hours later.

At 11 a.m. on the 11th day of the 11th month of 1918, the guns of Europe fell silent after more than four years of war. The problems of war were now replaced by the equally pressing problems of peace. Germany had asked for an armistice (cease-fire) in order to discuss a possible peace treaty. She had not surrendered but her soldiers were surrendering in hordes and her navy had mutinied. The Allies wanted to make sure that Germany would never go to war again. The eventual peace treaty redrew the map of Europe and forced Germany to pay massive damages to the Allies. German armed forces were reduced in size and strength and Germany lost a great deal of land and all of her overseas colonies.

DISPLACED PEOPLE
Many refugees, like these Lithuanians, were displaced during the war. The end of hostilities allowed thousands of refugees—mainly French, Belgians, Italians, and Serbians, whose lands had been occupied by the Central Powers—to return home to their newly liberated countries. In addition, there were as many as 6.5 million prisoners of war who needed to be repatriated. This complex task was finally achieved by the fall of 1919.

SPREADING THE NEWS
News of the armistice spread around the world in minutes. It was reported in newspapers and typed out in telegrams, while word-of-mouth spread the joyous news to each and every member of the local neighborhood.

VIVE LA PAIX!
In Paris (below), French, British, and American soldiers joined Parisians in an impromptu procession through the city. In London, women and children danced in the streets while their men prepared to return from the front. In Germany, the news was greeted with a mixture of shock and relief that the fighting was at last over.

SIGNING THE TREATY
These soldiers watching the signing of the Treaty of Versailles had waited a long time for this moment. The Allies first met their German counterparts in January 1919. The Americans wanted a fair and just treaty that guaranteed democracy and freedom to all people, while both France and, to a lesser extent, Britain wanted to keep Germany weak and divided. Negotiations almost broke down several times before a final agreement was reached in June 1919.

THE TREATY OF VERSAILLES
The peace treaty that ended the war was signed in the Hall of Mirrors in the Palace of Versailles near Paris on June 28, 1919. Sir William Orpen's painting shows the four Allied leaders watching the German delegates sign the treaty ending German imperial power in Europe, just 48 years after the German Empire had been proclaimed in the same hall.

THE PEACE TREATIES
The Treaty of Versailles was signed by representatives of the Allied powers and Germany. The Allies signed subsequent treaties elsewhere in Paris with Austria in September 1919, Bulgaria in November 1919, Turkey in April 1920, and Hungary in June 1920. By then, a new map of Europe had emerged.

The Treaty of Versailles

General Foch
Georges Clemenceau
David Lloyd George
Vittorio Orlando
Giorgio Sonnino

THE VICTORIOUS ALLIES
The negotiations in Paris were dominated by French premier Georges Clemenceau (supported by General Foch), British premier David Lloyd George, Italian premier Vittorio Orlando—seen here with his foreign minister, Giorgio Sonnino—and the US president Woodrow Wilson. Together, the Big Four, as they came to be known, thrashed out the main details of the peace settlement.

The cost of the war

THE COST OF World War I in human lives is unimaginable. More than 65 million men fought, of whom more than half were killed or injured—8 million killed, 2 million died of illness and disease, 21.2 million wounded, and 7.8 million taken prisoner or missing. In addition, about 6.6 million civilians perished. Among the combatant nations, with the exception of the US, there was barely a family that had not lost at least one son or brother; some had lost every male member. Entire towns and villages were wiped off the map, and fertile farmland was turned into deadly bogland. Financially, the economies of Europe were ruined, while the US emerged as a major world power. Not surprisingly, at the end of 1918, people hoped they would never again have to experience the slaughter and destruction they had lived through for the past four years.

ONE LIFE
A soldier stands on Pilckem Ridge during the Battle of Passchendaele in August 1917. The crudely made cross indicates a hastily dug grave, but many soldiers were engulfed by the mud and their graves remained unmarked.

THE UNKNOWN SOLDIER
Many of the dead were so badly disfigured that it was impossible to identify them. Plain crosses mark their graves. Thousands more just disappeared, presumed dead. Both France and Britain ceremoniously buried one unknown warrior—at the Arc de Triomphe, Paris, and Westminster Abbey, London.

AFTERCARE
The war left thousands of soldiers disfigured and disabled. Reconstructive surgery helped repair facial damage, while masks and prosthetics were used to cover horrible disfigurements. Artificial limbs gave many disabled soldiers some mobility. But the horrors of the war remained with many soldiers for the rest of their lives.

Some soldiers stayed in nursing homes for the rest of their lives

Many soldiers painted to pass the time

Background picture: Poppies in the battlefields of northern France

WAR MEMORIALS
The entire length of the Western Front is marked with graveyards and memorials to those who lost their lives in the war. The French national mausoleum and ossuary (burial vault) at Douaumont, Verdun (below), contains the remains of 130,000 unidentified French and German soldiers. There are 410 British cemeteries in the Somme valley alone.

Prussian Iron Cross

MEMENTOS
A profusion of flowers, including red Flanders poppies, grew along both sides of the Western Front. Soldiers, such as Private Jack Mudd of the 214 Battalion of the London Regiment (above), would press them as mementos to send home to their loved ones. Mudd sent this poppy to his wife, Lizzie, before he was killed, in 1917, in the Battle of Passchendaele. Canadian doctor, John McCrae, wrote the poem *In Flanders Fields* after tending wounded soldiers near Ypres in 1915. His mention of poppies in the poem inspired the British Legion to sell paper poppies to raise money for injured soldiers, and as a sign of remembrance for the dead.

Victoria Cross (V. C.)

FOR GALLANTRY
Every combatant nation awarded military and civilian medals to honor bravery. Five million Iron Crosses were given to German soldiers and their allies. Over two million Croix de Guerre were issued to French soldiers, military units, civilians, and towns, and 576 Victoria Crosses, Britain's highest award, were presented to British and Empire troops.

French *Croix de Guerre*

BITE-SIZED FACTS

The noise produced by artillery barrages and mines was incredibly loud. In 1917, explosives blowing up beneath the German lines on Messines Ridge at Ypres in Belgium could be heard in London, 140 miles (220 km) away.

Every British soldier was given army-issue boots in time to wear them in. From the Somme onward, each soldier also had his own steel helmet. Specialized items, such as rubber wading boots, were kept as community property—handed from one unit to another.

Map of Europe in 1914 by Walter Trier

British Army clothing, left to right: a warm coat for transport drivers; a flameproof suit for flame thrower operators; winter camouflage for trench raiding; and flying clothing

Flame throwers were first used by the Germans. They fired jets of flame as far as 130 ft (40 m).

Russia had the largest army. It mobilized 12 million troops during the course of the war. More than three-quarters were killed, wounded, or went missing in action.

At first British tanks were split into "males" and "females." Male tanks had cannons, while females had heavy machine guns.

The first prototype tank, "Little Willie," was built in 1915. It carried a crew of three and had a top speed of 3 mph (4.8 kph).

Tunnelers laid mines on the Western Front. Sometimes underground fights broke out, if they dug into an enemy tunnel by mistake.

Food was prepared in field kitchens that could be several miles behind the front line. It was impossible to take transport trucks into the trench, so food was carried to the front on foot.

Filling a Thermos container that kept the food hot

Prague-born Walter Trier (1890–1951) produced political cartoons. One famous work shows Europe in 1914 on the eve of World War I, with the national leaders squabbling and threatening each other.

The Pool of Peace is a 40-ft (12-m) deep lake near Messines, Belgium. It fills a crater made in 1917 when the British detonated a mine containing 44 tons (41,325 kg) of explosives.

Some soldiers wore knitted helmets called balaclavas to stay warm in winter. Balaclavas are named after the battle where they were first worn—the Battle of Balaclava, which took place during the Crimean War (1854).

A German messenger dog laying telegraph wire

Messenger dogs carried orders to the front line in capsules strapped to their bodies. Dogs also helped military communications in another way—some of them were trained to lay down telegraph wire!

QUESTIONS AND ANSWERS

Modern-day camouflage

Q Who was "Big Bertha"?

A Big Bertha was a 47-ton (43,700-kg) howitzer used by the Germans in World War I. Its designer, Gustav Krupp, named the weapon after his wife. Big Bertha was more mobile than the previous 16½-in (420-mm) howitzer; it could be transported to its firing position by tractor. Even so, it took its crew of 200 men six hours or more to assemble it. Big Bertha was a formidable weapon. It could fire a 2,050-lb (930-kg) shell a distance of over 9 miles (15 km). Big Bertha's first successes were at Liege in Belgium. The 12 forts ringing the city were destroyed in three days.

Q Why did soldiers keep animals?

A Most animals that traveled with the army had a job to do. Mules, horses, and camels were kept as draft or pack animals to transport heavy supplies.

Soldiers with their rabbits and chickens

Messenger dogs and pigeons carried important communications. Away from the front line, some soldiers kept animals for food—rabbits for the cooking pot or hens for their eggs. Some animals were kept simply to keep up morale. Dogs, for example, were popular, but one group of South African soldiers had an impala as their lucky mascot!

Q How did soldiers camouflage themselves?

A World War I was the first major conflict in which soldiers made use of camouflage. They wore khaki uniforms that blended in with the background. Some snipers made camouflaged suits out of painted sacking. Steel helmets were often painted with matte paint mixed with sand or sawdust so that they would not reflect the light; other times they were smeared with mud or covered with sacking from sandbags. Soldiers also used sacking or netting to hide their equipment from the reconnaissance aircraft patrolling the skies, but blending in was not the only camouflage possibility. The disruptive patterns painted on to battleships also worked—just as a zebra's stripes can confuse a lion.

Q How did soldiers know when to put on their gas masks?

A There were soldiers on lookout duty night and day. These sentries used whatever they could find to raise the alarm—bells, rattles, whistles, or just their own voice. When the soldiers heard the alarm they put on their gas masks as quickly as they could—hopefully, before the deadly gas drifted toward the trench.

Q Why were tanks called tanks?

A While it was being developed, the tank was known as a "landship." However, there were fears that this name was too obvious. Before long, a German spy might become curious about why so many of these objects were being produced, and the Germans might catch on to the new invention. The British had to come up with a believable name. They decided that, with its rectangular bodyshape, perhaps it could be passed off as a water storage tank. At first, they chose the name "water carrier"—until someone noticed that this would be abbreviated to "WC," the abbreviation for "water closet," or toilet. In the end, they decided on "tank" instead.

Sentry wears mask to protect from gas attack

Metal bell sounds the alarm

A sentry on duty

So many people played an important role in planning or fighting World War I. It is impossible to cover them all, but here are a few of them, together with a checklist of some of the key battle sites.

IMPORTANT PERSONALITIES

Russian General Brusilov

Alexei Brusilov (1853–1926)
With his "Bru silov offensive" of 1916, General Brusilov broke Austro-Hungarian lines. He took command of Russian armies on the Eastern Front in 1917.

Luigi Cadorna (1850–1928)
The general in charge of the Italian army was Luigi Cadorna. His only success was the recapture of Gorizia in 1916.

Ferdinand Foch (1851–1929)
Artillery specialist Ferdinand Foch successfully led the French at the Marne. By 1918 he was coordinating all the Allied forces on the Western Front.

Anthony Fokker (1890–1939)
Dutch designer Anthony Fokker developed the first fighter plane with a forward-facing synchronized machine gun. His Fokker Eindecker gave Germany the edge in the early part of the war. Fokker produced 40 different aircrafts during the war.

René Fonck (1894–1953)
Frenchman René Fonck was the Allies' most successful fighter pilot. He shot down 75 enemy planes.

Douglas Haig (1861–1928)
The general in charge of British troops on the Western Front was Sir Douglas Haig. He ordered the offensives at the Somme and Passchendaele, as well as the final, successful Allied offensive.

Paul von Hindenburg (1847–1934)
Early in the war, Paul von Hindenburg successfully led the Germans against the Russians. By 1916, he commanded all German land forces. His Hindenburg Line, created in 1917, withstood attack until 1918.

Joseph Joffre (1852–1931)
When the war broke out, Joseph Joffre became Commander of the French army. He planned attacks on the Western Front but, after heavy losses, was replaced in 1916.

T. E. Lawrence (1888–1935)
Known as Lawrence of Arabia, T. E. Lawrence worked for Allied intelligence in the Middle East. He led an Arab revolt against the Turks, which he wrote about in his book *The Seven Pillars of Wisdom*.

President Raymond Poincaré of France *General Sir Douglas Haig*

Rittmeister von Richthofen (1892–1918)
Known as the Red Baron, this German aviator shot down 80 planes—more than any other World War I pilot. He died after being shot down near Amiens.

Maximilian von Spee (1861–1914)
German admiral Maximilian von Spee sank two British cruisers off Chile. He died when his own ship, the *Scharnhorst*, went down near the Falkland Islands.

Gabriel Voisin (1880–1973)
French-born Gabriel Voisin was an aircraft designer. He is famous for his Voisin III (the first Allied plane to shoot down an enemy) and his Voisin V bomber, which was armed with a cannon.

Margaretha Zelle (1876–1917)
Dutch-born Margaretha Zelle was better known as Mata Hari. She always denied being a double agent, but it is possible that she spied for both the French and Germans. The French executed her in 1917.

Propeller rotation was synchronized with gunfire

Anthony Fokker with his Fokker DI aircraft

Aircraft designer Gabriel Voisin (right)

MAJOR BATTLES

Tanks pass through Meaulte, France, during the Amiens offensive

AMIENS
In August 1918, General Rawlinson led his successful Allied offensive to recapture the Amiens Line. On the first day, the Allies advanced 7½ miles (12 km).

CAMBRAI
General Haig took the Germans by surprise in November 1917 when he attacked them at Cambrai, France. At first, the Allies gained good ground, but within two weeks the Germans had regained their position. The estimated casualties were 45,000 British soldiers and 50,000 Germans.

GAZA
General Dobell led a British attack on Turkish-held Gaza in March 1917. The port was a strategic target, on the way to Palestine. The British took the Turks by surprise, but were soon forced to retreat. They eventually captured Gaza in November, after weakening its defenses with bombardment from offshore ships.

A British dressing station at Cambrai

HELIGOLAND BIGHT
In August 1914, two British light cruisers and 25 destroyers attacked German ships near the naval base on Heligoland in the North Sea. In the battle that followed, the British sank three cruisers and a destroyer.

JUTLAND
May 1916 saw the war's only major sea battle, off the Danish coast of Jutland. Both sides claimed victory. The Germans inflicted the heaviest losses, but the British had maintained control of the North Sea.

The Retreat from Mons (1927) by Lady Elizabeth Butler

MONS
The British Expeditionary Force met the advancing German army at Mons, France, in August 1914. Although the Germans suffered heavy losses, they managed to force back the British to the Marne River.

PASSCHENDAELE
The Battle of Passchendaele, Belgium, began in July 1917. First, the Allies spent 10 days bombarding the Germans. Then they advanced, but were slowed down by torrential rains. The Allies finally took the ridge of Passchendaele in November.

SOMME
July 1916 saw the start of the Battle of the Somme, France. On the first day, the British suffered 58,000 casualties. Despite this, the Allies continued their offensive until November. When it was finally called off, the Allies had suffered 620,000 casualties and the Germans an estimated 500,000 casualties.

VERDUN
The Germans attacked the French garrison town of Verdun in February 1916. Initially they outnumbered the French five to one, but they failed to take the town. The battle ran on for 10 months and nearly a million men lost their lives.

VITTORIO-VENETO
One of the last offensives of the war was when the Italians recaptured Vittorio-Veneto on October 29, 1918. The Austro-Hungarian forces had retreated the day before.

YPRES
The Belgian town of Ypres was taken by the Germans in August 1914, but the British recaptured it in October. During the failed German counterattack, the British forces were decimated. A second battle of Ypres took place in April and May 1915 and a third, Passchendaele, in 1917.

A British field kitchen at the Somme, 1916

Find out more

THERE ARE MANY WAYS you can find out more about World War I. Ask older generations of your family if they remember stories about relatives who fought in the war. There are personal accounts online, too, plus lots of other information. Try your library for special books on the topic and visit war museums. In addition to vast collections of fascinating objects, these often have interactive displays. Television documentaries also bring the war to life with real or reconstructed footage. Finally, remember there is a wealth of old war movies that will give you a feel for what life was like.

Poppy symbolizes remembrance

REMEMBRANCE DAY
Everyone can play a part in commemorating the sacrifices of soldiers and civilians during World War I. Each year, on the Sunday nearest to November 11, services are held at local and national war memorials.

THE TANK MUSEUM
Fans of tracked vehicles should head to Bovington, Dorset, England, to see the world's largest tank collection. A key attraction is the first tank prototype, Little Willie. The museum also has a program of special events.

ARC DE TRIOMPHE
Originally built by Napoleon to celebrate the victories of his armies, the Arc de Triomphe in Paris, France, now keeps the memory of the millions of soldiers killed in World War I. Its flame of remembrance is rekindled each day and, in November 1920, the body of an unknown soldier was buried under the monument. He is there to symbolize the soldiers who died in the war.

Anzac veteran wears wartime medals and decorations

French tricolor (national flag) is flown each year on November 11

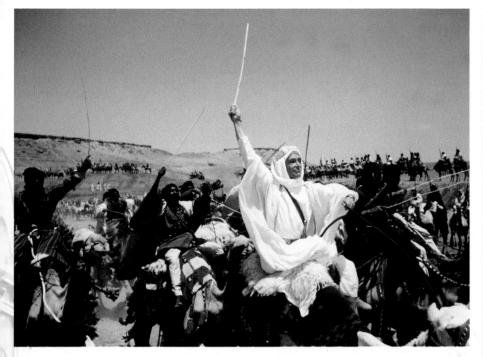

WAR MOVIES

A great many movies have been made about the events of World War I. They may not always be based on solid facts, but they are an entertaining way to get a flavor of the time and events. One of the best is *Lawrence of Arabia* (1962). Directed by David Lean, it starred Peter O'Toole (shown above) in the title role.

USEFUL WEBSITES

- Easy-to-navigate site featuring timelines, maps, photographs, biographies, and more:
  www.worldwars.com
- A companion website to the PSB series on World War I, including multimedia effects:
  www.pbs.org/greatwar
- Extensive multimedia site with propaganda posters, vintage film and audio, and in-depth historical information:
  www.firstworldwar.com

Places to visit

SMITHSONIAN INSTITUTION, WASHINGTON, D.C.
Explore the myths and realities of World War I combat. On exhibit are actual aircraft that took to the skies during World War I.

LIBERTY MEMORIAL MUSEUM, KANSAS CITY, MISSOURI
The only public mueseum in the United States dedicated solely to the history of World War I. Historical items in the collection include gas masks, letters and postcards from the field, memorial paintings, and other artifacts from World War I.

THE US AIR FORCE (USAF) MUSEUM, DAYTON, OHIO
The history gallery provides an overview of the US Army Air Service involvement in World War I. The gallery supports actual displays of World War I aircraft at the largest military aviation museum in the world.

PARRIS ISLAND MUSEUM, PARRIS ISLAND, SOUTH CAROLINA
Marines were among the first foces to be sent to France during World War I. This World War I exhibit features foreign and domestic apparel, equipment, and weapons, including trench knives, a Maxim water-cooler machine gun, and a Model 1908 Luger used by the Germans.

IMPERIAL WAR MUSEUM, LONDON, ENGLAND
See a World War I tank, or visit a dedicated gallery with firearms, uniforms, posters, medals, and other memorabilia in themed areas. The Trench Experience exhibit features sights, sounds, and smells the bring the Battle of the Somme to life.

Life-size model shows army doctor dressing wounds

Sculpture shows parents mourning the loss of their son

WAR MONUMENT

Many artists and writers were so horrified or moved by the war that they felt compelled to express these feelings in their work. German sculptor Kathe Kollwitz (1867–1945) made this statue for the German war cemetery at Roggevelde, Belgium. Her own son, Peter, is buried there.

IMPERIAL WAR MUSEUM

This exhibit is part of the Trench Experience at the Imperial War Museum, London, England. A combination of lights, sounds, and smells helps visitors to understand just how terrifying and disorientating trench life was.

Glossary

Nurses wheel convalescent soldiers around the hospital grounds

ABDICATE Give up office or power.

ALLIANCE A group of allies, who have agreed to act in cooperation. Allied countries often set out their shared goals in an official treaty.

ALTITUDE Height above sea level.

AMMUNITION Bullets and shells fired from weapons.

AMPUTATION Surgical removal of a body part, such as an arm or leg.

ANZAC Member of the Australian and New Zealand Army Corps.

ARMISTICE End of hostilities. Armistice Day, now known as Remembrance Sunday in Europe, is commemorated each year on the Sunday closest to November 11.

ARMS RACE Competition between nations to build up weaponry, or armaments.

ARTILLERY Armed forces that use heavy weapons, such as cannons.

ASSASSINATION The murder of someone for political purposes.

BATTERY The place where a cannon, or other form of artillery, is positioned.

BAYONET A blade fixed to a rifle or other firearm. The bayonet can be used to stab the enemy when fighting at close quarters.

BULLY BEEF Another name for corned beef.

BUNKER An underground bomb shelter.

BUTTON STICK Metal slide used to protect a soldier's uniform from polish when shining their buttons.

CAMOUFLAGE Coloring designed to blend in with the background. During World War I, this was mostly limited to attempts to conceal gun positions, although some soldiers blackened their faces before night patrols and snipers wore camouflaged suits.

CAVALRY Originally, soldiers on horseback, but the term came to mean soldiers using motorized transportation, such as tanks.

CLIP A means of carrying and rapidly loading rifle ammunition.

COLONY A dependency, or place, that is ruled by a foreign nation.

CONSCIENTIOUS OBJECTOR Someone who refuses to fight for moral reasons.

CONSCRIPT Someone who is forced by law to fight in the army.

CONSCRIPTION Making people fight in the army.

Small box respirator gas mask

CONVALESCENT Someone who has been seriously injured or sick and is slowly recovering.

CONVOY Merchant ships traveling together, protected by a naval escort.

CREEPING BARRAGE A line of artillery fire creeping ahead of an infantry advance.

CRYPTOGRAPHY The study and creation of secret codes.

DETONATE To explode or cause to explode.

DYSENTERY An infection of the intestines that causes diarrhea and bloody feces.

EMPLACEMENT A mound or platform from which guns are fired.

ENDEMIC Found in a particular area, or among a certain group of people.

ENLIST Call or sign up to the armed forces.

ENTENTE A friendly agreement or informal alliance between nations.

An intelligence officer inspects aerial photographs of enemy trenches

EVACUATION Moving people away from a place where they are in danger.

FLOTILLA A fleet or group of small ships.

FRONT LINE The border between enemy territories, where the fighting is.

FUSELAGE The body of an airplane.

GAS In the context of war, "gas" means a poisonous gas, such as chlorine, used as a weapon to choke, blind, or kill the enemy.

GRENADE A small bomb that is hurled by hand.

GUERRILLA A soldier in a guerrilla army— a small-scale outfit that practises sabotage and hit-and-run attacks. Guerrilla comes from the Spanish for "small war."

KNOT A unit for measuring a ship's speed. One knot equals 1.15 mph (1.85 kph).

MACHINE GUN An automatic gun that fires bullets in rapid succession.

MEDICAL ORDERLY A soldier with some medical training, who works in an army medical establishment.

MESS TIN A soldier's cooking pot.

MINE A large underground chamber packed with explosives, placed under enemy lines by tunnelers.

MOBILIZATION Preparation of troops for active service.

MORALE Strength of purpose, confidence, or faith.

MORSE CODE A code where each letter of the alphabet is represented by a sequence of dots and dashes, or by long or short signals of light or sound. It is named after its inventor, Samuel Morse (1791–1872).

MUNITIONS Stores of weapons and other military equipment.

NEUTRALITY The state of not taking sides.

NO-MAN'S-LAND An area of land between two opposing forces, that has not been captured by either side.

NONCOMBATANT Someone connected with the army but not there to fight, for example a chaplain or army doctor.

PERISCOPE A device that uses mirrors to allow the user to see things that are not in his or her direct line of sight.

PICKET A metal stake used to tether an entanglement—that is, a tangle of barbed wire used to fortify the front-row trenches.

POSTHUMOUSLY After death.

PROPAGANDA Information intended to convince people of a particular viewpoint. It may take the form of posters, broadcasts, or air-dropped leaflets, for example.

PUTTEE A strip of cloth wound around the lower part of the leg.

RECONNAISSANCE Taking a preliminary look at an area before sending in troops, usually in order to locate the enemy.

RECONNOITER To survey an area in preparation for a military advance.

German stereoscopic periscope

RECRUIT Someone who is enlisted into the army.

REGULAR FORCES Soldiers who already belong to the army, rather than conscripts.

RESERVE FORCES People who are not part of the regular army but have received some military training, and are ready to be the first extra troops mobilized in an emergency.

RESPIRATOR A device worn over the face to prevent the wearer from breathing in poison gas.

RIFLE A long-barreled gun, fired from shoulder level.

SEAPLANE An aircraft equipped with floats or skis so that it can land on or take off from water.

SHELL An explosive device that is fired, for example, from a cannon.

SHELLSHOCK Mental strain or illness suffered by a soldier who has fought in a war.

SHRAPNEL A type of antipersonnel projectile that contained small shot or spherical bullets, usually of lead, along with an explosive charge to scatter the shot.

TELEGRAPH A communications device that transmits messages by means of electrical signals along a wire.

TERRORIST Someone who commits violent acts to bring about or draw attention to their political goals.

TORPEDO A self-propelled underwater missile that can be fired from a boat or submarine.

TRENCH A ditch dug by soldiers that gives some protection against enemy fire.

TRUCE An agreement to stop fighting.

U-BOAT A German submarine.

ULTIMATUM A final demand, which, if it is not met, will result in serious consequences and a total breakdown of communication.

WAR BOND A certificate issued by a government in return for the investment of a sum of money. The money raised by the bonds helps pay for the war. It is repaid later with interest.

WAR OF ATTRITION Continuously attacking to wear down the enemy.

WIRELESS A communications device that sends messages as radio signals.

TOGETHER WE WIN

UNITED STATES SHIPPING BOARD ———— EMERGENCY FLEET CORPORATION

An American propaganda poster

HOWITZER A short gun that fired high.

INCENDIARY Describes a bomb, bullet, or other device designed to cause fire.

INFANTRY Foot soldiers.

INTELLIGENCE Useful military or political information, or the spies that gather it.

INTERROGATE Question someone aggressively.

British .303-in (7.7-mm) Maxim Mark 3 medium machine gun, c. 1902